The Topic Dictionary

THE TOPIC DICTIONARY

English words and idioms.
S.M. Bennett and T.G. van Veen

Illustrated by Jan Sanders

Nelson

THOMAS NELSON & SONS LIMITED
Nelson House, Mayfield Road,
Walton-on-Thames, Surrey KT12 5PL,
England.

P.O. Box 18123,
Nairobi,
Kenya.

116-D, JTC Factory Building,
Lorong 3, Geylang Square,
Singapore 1438.

THOMAS NELSON AUSTRALIA PTY LIMITED,
19–39 Jeffcott Street,
West Melbourne, Victoria 3003,
Australia.

NELSON CANADA LIMITED,
81 Curlew Drive, Don Mills,
Ontario M3A 2R1,
Canada.

THOMAS NELSON (HONG KONG) LIMITED,
Watson Estate, Block A, 13 Floor,
Watson Road, Causeway Bay,
Hong Kong.

THOMAS NELSON (NIGERIA) LIMITED,
8 Ilupeju Bypass, PMB 21303,
Ikeja, Lagos,
Nigeria.

© Thomas Nelson and Sons Ltd 1981
First published by Meulenhoff Educatief

ISBN 0-17-555331-9

NCN 759-8945

Printed in Hong Kong

Introduction

The **Topic Dictionary** is designed to help the learner of English build up and consolidate a knowledge of words and idioms through practice. Some 3,300 words are introduced in topic areas which group them together by subject. All items from the Threshold level and 90 irregular verbs are included together with other core vocabulary which should be made familiar to students in the course of their studies.

A list of 300 basic words is given on p. 1 and students should be familiar with these words before beginning to use the **Topic Dictionary.**

In the classroom
The **Topic Dictionary** is arranged in word-fields with a progression through the units making it easy for the teacher to work systematically through the book, topic by topic. For students whose need is consolidation work there is also great potential for random selection by topic.

The illustrations reinforce the introduction of items and provide stimuli for extending vocabulary work. The question-and-answer format lends itself to oral and written practice and checking of vocabulary.

The word-field arrangement makes the **Topic Dictionary** a useful tool for teaching vocabulary for related reading and writing tasks.

Self-Study
Students who want to use the **Topic Dictionary** without a teacher will find that the question-and-answer format provides an instant check. The pages are arranged so that students can cover the answers and test themselves.

The arrangement by topic provides easy access and helps to build vocabulary quickly, making the dictionary easy and fun to use.

Contents

1 Flying is fun 2
2 Round the world in one lesson 6
3 Wildlife 11
4 Let's go to town 15
5 Going into the countryside 19
6 What's your job? 25
7 Stop… thief! 29
8 At the pub 32
9 At school 36
10 What's on tonight? 41
11 My home is my castle 45
12 What's your favourite sport? 49
13 A day at the races 54
14 A pop concert 58
15 Casting your vote 62
16 At church 65
17 At a fashion-parade 70
18 A talk about history 75
19 A birthday party 80
20 A picnic in the woods 84
21 A holiday at the seaside 87
22 Meeting friends 90
23 An accident 94
24 In the artist's studio 97
25 Do you like sailing? 101
26 A portrait 106
27 At the Post Office 112
28 Shopping 115
29 Join the Army 119
30 Home is home 124
31 I'm a sentence 131
32 The end of the journey 134
Index 138

Alphabetic list of the 300 basic English words. Students should be familiar with these words before using the Topic Dictionary.

---

a about across afraid after again all almost already always am an and another any apple are as ask at away

baby back bad bag ball be because bed been before beside best big bird black blue book box boy bring bus but by bye-bye

call came can car cat children chips come cool could cow cup

day daughter dead dear did dine dinner dish do dog doll don't door down

eat egg end ever every except

false fare farm fast father fell find first fish five fly for four found from fun

gave get girl give go going good got grass green grey

had hand has hat have he head help her here hill him his home hope horse house how hunger

I ice if in into is it

jam jump just

keep know

last later lazy left let letter like little live long look

made make man many market may me men milk Miss moment money more morning mother Mr. Mrs. much must my

name nationality never new next night not nothing no now

of off old on once one only open or other our out over own

petrol picture pig place plan plastic play pot put

rabbit ran read real red right road room round run

said sat saw say school sea see she shirt shop should since sing sister sit so some soon stop sound still strange street strong sun

table take tall tea tell test than that the their them then there these they thing think this three time to today too top toy train tree true two

under until up us

very

wait walk want was watch water we weak well went were what when where white which why will winter wish with without who whose woman work would wrong

year yes you your

+ names of days of the week and months of the year.

from 'Key words to literacy', J. McNally & W. Murray. The Schoolmaster Publishing Company Ltd., London.

1 Flying is fun

B What do you see first when you drive to an airport?
   First you enter the…
   When you want to fly you have to buy a…
   You can buy your ticket at the …
   Planes land and start on a…
   The people who work in the plane are called the …
   The pilot in charge of the plane is also called the …
   When you are going to fly you are one of the …

B the airport buildings
   departure lounge
   ticket
   booking-office
   runway
   crew
   captain
   passengers

Looking after the passengers is the task of the …   airhostess
When a plane touches the runway we call that the …   landing
When a plane departs we say …   the plane takes off
Another word for the start of a plane is the …   take-off
In a plane you sit in…   seats
When the plane takes off you have to…   fasten your seat-belts
Before you enter another country you must pass through
the…   customs

C *Make your choice:*   C .

The airhostess/pilot takes care of you when you are on board
a plane.   the airhostess
The engineer/the pilot flies the plane.   the pilot
During the take-off the passengers must remain in their
seats/chairs.   in their seats
A plane is repaired in a hangar/garage.   in a hangar

D *Give the three principal forms of the following verbs:*   D

to take [off]   take – took – taken
to fly   fly – flew – flown
to buy   buy – bought – bought

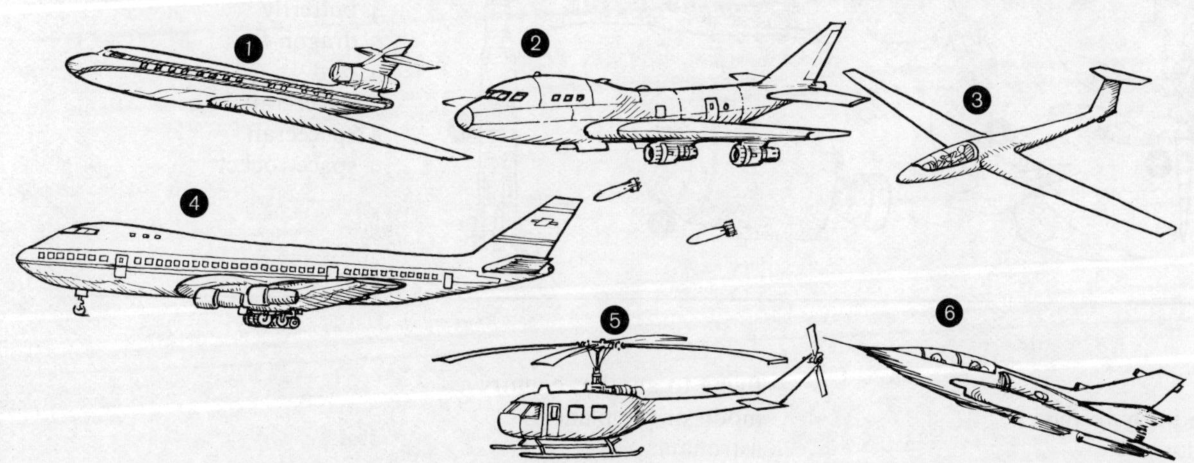

E *Some kinds of planes
[aircraft]*
1 passenger-plane
2 bomber
3 glider
4 jumbo jet
5 helicopter
6 fighter

F *Make nouns from:*

to land	landing
to start	start
to arrive	arrival
to fly	flight
to take off	take-off
to depart	departure

G When somebody captures a plane we call it… — hijacking
The man who does so is a… — hijacker
With a parachute you can safely… — jump out of a plane
When a plane is out of control and hits the ground we speak of a… — crash
To find his way in bad weather the pilot uses… — radio and radar
Aviation is a term for… — everything to do with the flying of aircraft

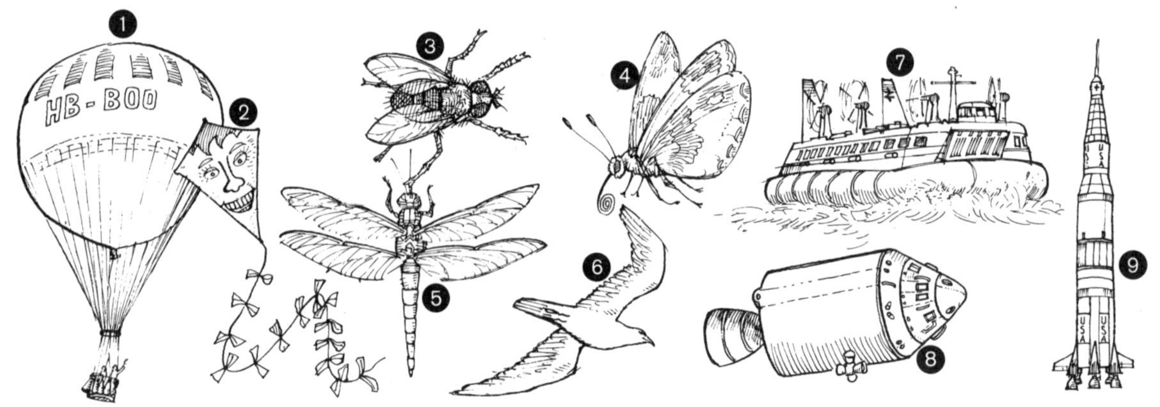

H *They can fly too*
1 balloon
2 kite
3 fly
4 butterfly
5 dragon-fly
6 bird
7 hovercraft
8 spacecraft
9 space rocket

I *Flight to the moon*
Flying abroad means… — flying to another country
In a spacecraft it is possible to fly to the… — moon or the planets
People who do so are called… — astronauts

Our planet is called…

The planets and stars are in the…

Around the earth there is an…

To breathe we need…

Missiles are often used in…

Rockets are used to launch…

earth

universe

atmosphere

oxygen

wartime

spacecraft and missiles

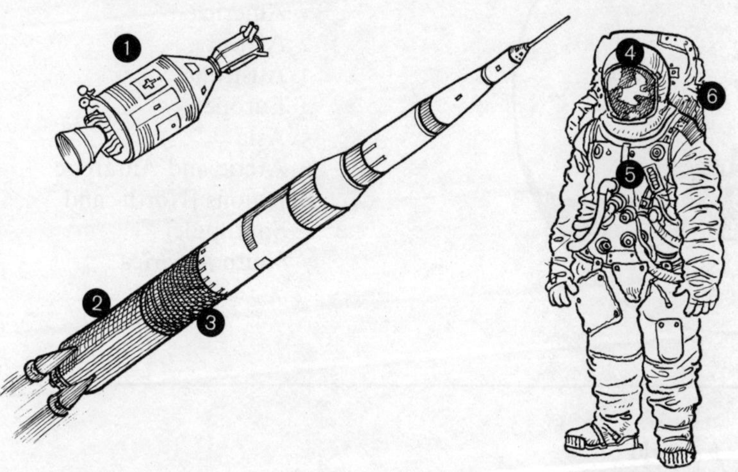

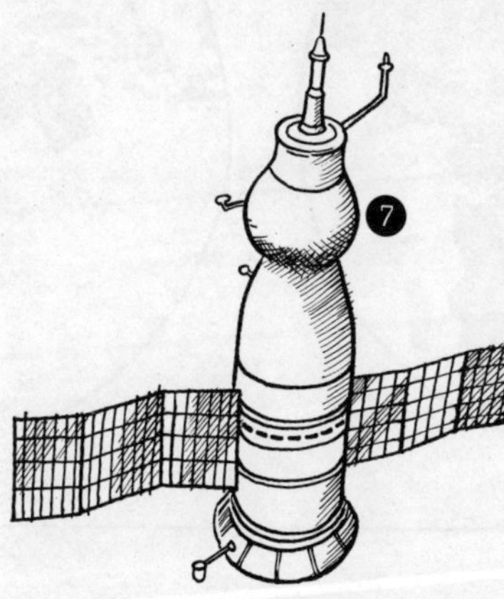

J *A spacecraft*
1 capsule
2 first stage
3 fuel
4 space-helmet
5 space-suit
6 oxygen pack
7 space-station

K *Give the opposite of:*
to arrive
to take off
a safe landing

L Songs and poems about the moon are often…

Here is a song about space!
Hey, Mr. Spaceman/Won't you please take me along?/
I won't do anything wrong/Hey, Spaceman/Won't you please
take me along for a ride?

Chorus part. Pop group: The Byrds.

K

to depart
to land
a crash landing

L romantic songs and poems

2 Round the world in one lesson

A *Parts of the world/
continents*
1 America
2 Africa
3 Australia
4 Europe
5 Asia
6 Arctic and Antarctic regions [North- and Southpole]
7 South America

B By plane we can fly to most places in the …
We say then that we are going on a…
When we go by boat we call it a…
A journey which is not so long we call a…
Going to other places is called…
What part of the world do Europeans live in?
People who live in America/Africa/Australia/Asia are called…
When English people say 'He lives on the Continent' they mean…

B world
journey
voyage
trip
travelling
Europe
Americans/Africans/Australians/Asians

he lives on the continent of Europe

C Name some countries where they speak English.

We say then that these people speak English as their…
We can also say that English is their…

C England [Britain]/Australia/The U.S.A. [United States of America]/New-Zealand/parts of Canada
native language
mother tongue

D *Ways of travelling*
   You can travel…

   Standing by the roadside trying to get a lift is called…
   When you travel this way you are a…
   When you want to travel by boat, bus, train or plane you
   must buy a…
   'To book' means to…

E Between the continents there are…
   Name some oceans.
   Oceans are…
   Between Holland and England is the…
   Some other seas in Europe are:

   The small strip of water between France and England is
   called the…
   An important English river is the…
   A well-known river in Germany is the…
   One of the most important rivers in France is the…
   In Scotland lakes are called…

F Name the four main points of the compass…
   In what part of Great Britain do we find Scotland?
   In what part of England is the isle of Wight?
   An adjective derived from 'east' is…
   A cowboy film they sometimes call a…
   The country to the east of the Netherlands is called…
   Countries are separated from each other by…

G *Name the principal forms of:*
   to build
   to swim
   to find
   to dig

D
on foot/by bike/by car/by train [by rail]/by boat/by plane/
on horseback
hitch-hiking
hitch-hiker

ticket
reserve a place

E oceans
Atlantic/Pacific/Indian Ocean/Arctic/Antarctic
large seas
North Sea
the Mediterranean/the Baltic/the Irish Sea/
the White Sea

English Channel
Thames
Rhine
Seine
lochs [Loch Ness]

F north/east/south/west
in the northern part
in the southern part
eastern
western
Germany
frontiers/borders

G

build – built – built
swim – swam – swum
find – found – found
dig – dug – dug

 Countries of Europe and their inhabitants [*people who live in these*
countries]
What is the name of the countries you see on the map and
which people live there?

1	England	the English
2	Norway	the Norwegians
3	Finland	the Finns
4	Denmark	the Danes
5	Russia	the Russians
6	Sweden	the Swedes
7	Belgium	the Belgians
8	The Netherlands	the Dutch
9	Germany	the Germans
10	Poland	the Poles
11	France	the French
12	Spain	the Spaniards
13	Portugal	the Portuguese
14	Switzerland	the Swiss
15	Austria	the Austrians
16	Italy	the Italians
17	Greece	the Greeks
18	Ireland	the Irish
19	Turkey	the Turks

I Now describe what you sec in each country.

I
1 an English hat
2 Norwegian wool
3 Finnish wood
4 Danish butter
5 Russian corn
6 a Swedish lake
7 Belgian glass
8 Dutch cheese
9 a German river
10 Polish person
11 French wine
12 Spanish sherry
13 Portuguese fishermen
14 Swiss mountains
15 Austrian house
16 Italian food [spaghetti]
17 Greek temple
18 Irish whiskey
19 a Turkish carpet

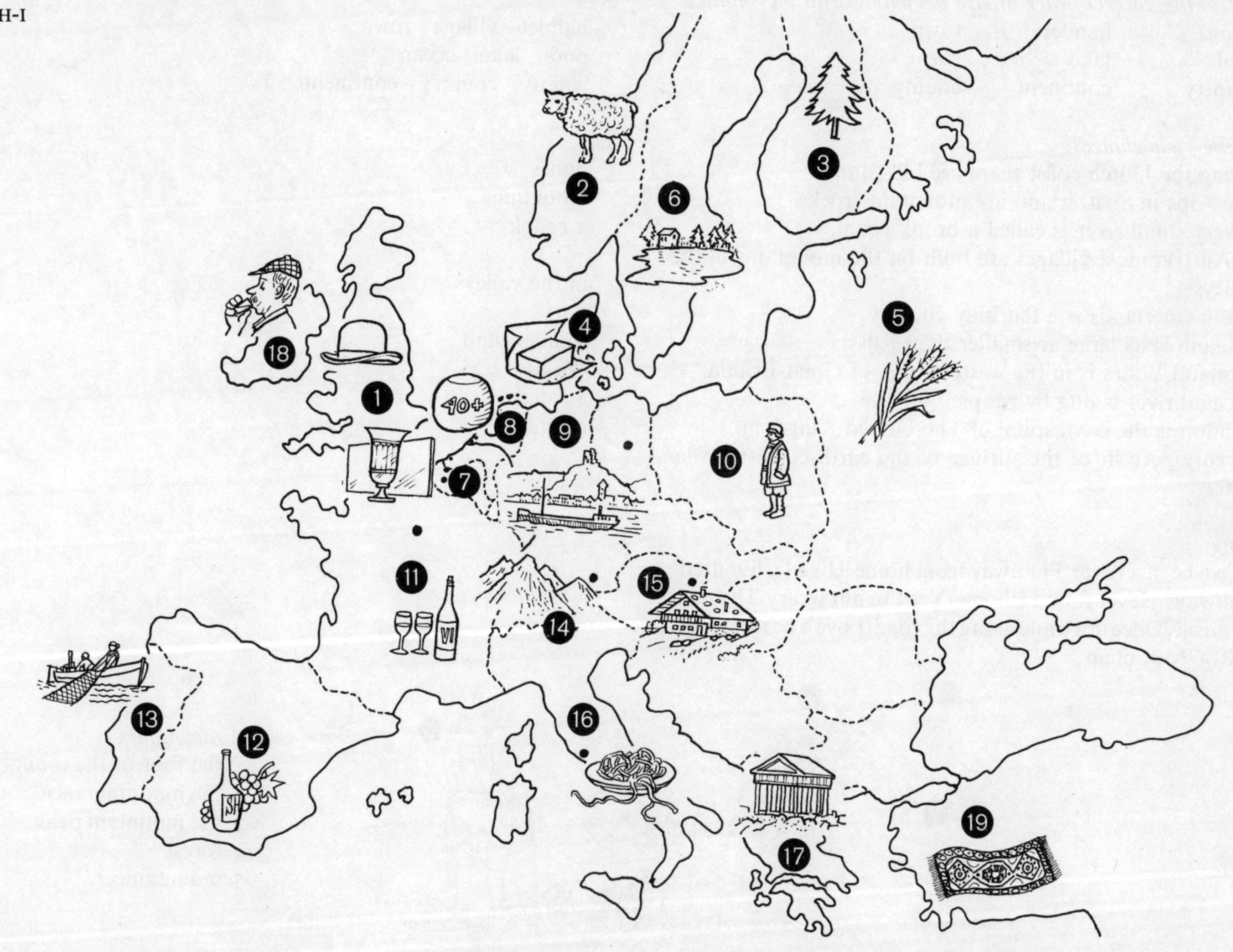

J The capital cities of: England/Norway/Finland/Denmark/
Russia/Sweden/Belgium/the Netherlands/Germany/Poland/
France/Spain/Portugal/Switzerland/Austria/Italy/Greece/
are…

J London/Oslo/Helsinki/Copenhagen/Moscow/Stockholm/
Brussels/the Hague/Bonn/Warsaw/Paris/Madrid/Lisbon/
Geneva/Vienna/Rome/Athens

K *Put in the correct order of size beginning with the smallest:*

village   hamlet   town
pool   lake   ocean
country   continent   county

K

hamlet – village – town
pool – lake – ocean
county – country – continent

L *Make your choice!*
Along the Dutch coast there are hills/dunes.
The Alps in Switzerland are mountains/rocks.
A very small river is called a brook/canal.
In Austria most villages are built on the mountains/in the valleys.
The Netherlands is a flat/hilly country.
Belgium is as large as/smaller than Russia.
Scotland/Wales is in the western part of Great Britain.
A canal/river is dug by people.
London is the city/capital of The United Kingdom.
Seventy percent of the surface of the earth consists of land/water.

L

dunes
mountains
a brook

in the valleys
flat
smaller than
Wales
a canal
capital

water

M *Song*
I have been a rover/Far away from home/Hiked a hundred
highways/Never found a home/Yet I'm not weary/The reason
is you see/Once in a while along the road/Love's been good to me.
   Rod McCuhan

N *A mountain*
   1 the foot of the mountain
   2 the mountain face
   3 the mountain peak
   4 forest
   5 mountaineer

O *Expressions*
You can't make water flow up-hill.
To make a mountain out of a mole-hill.

O *Meaning*
You can't make the impossible happen.
To make small troubles more important than they are
[to exaggerate].

3 Wildlife

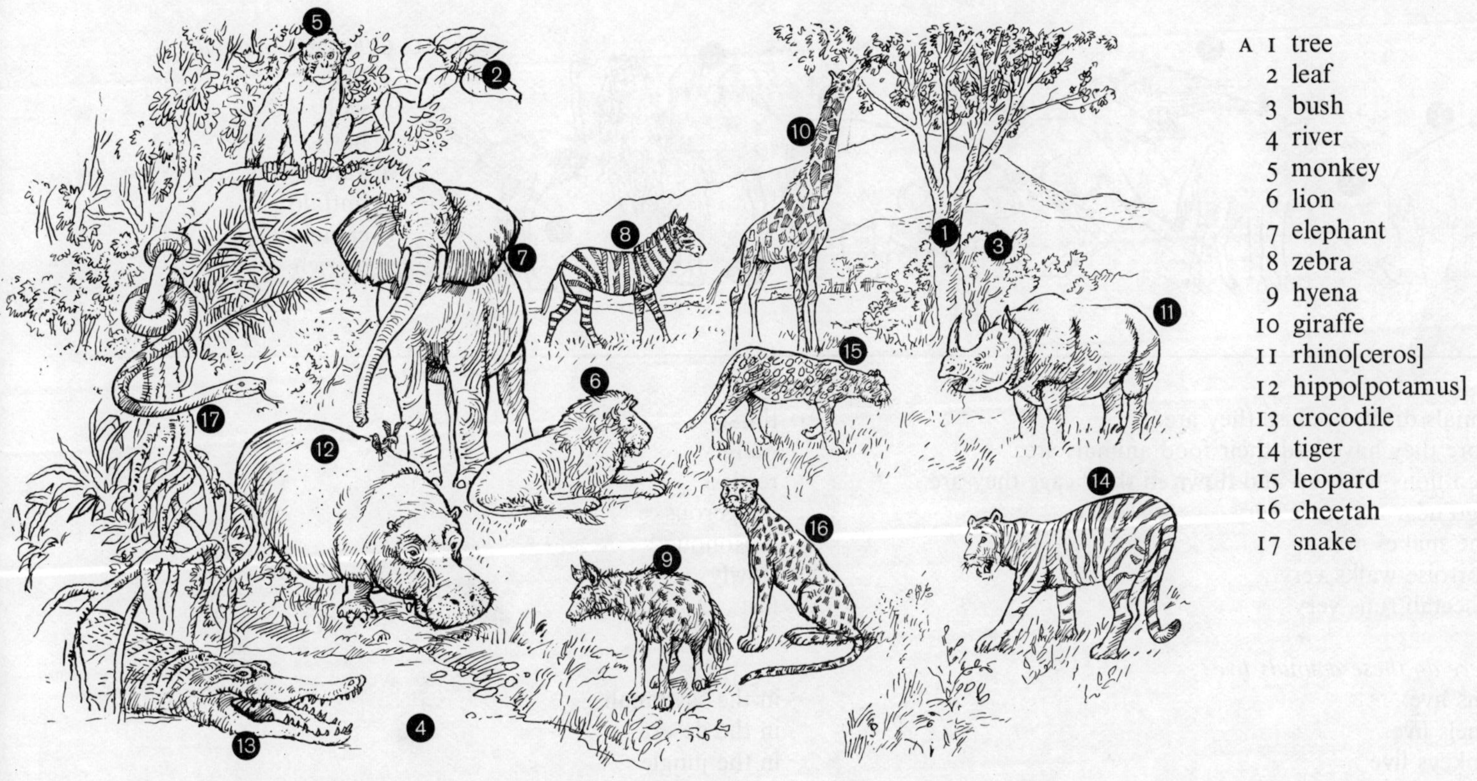

B	B
What do we call animals that kill other animals for food?	beasts of prey/predatory animals
Lions and jaguars are members of the…	cat family
We say that predatory animals live…	on other animals
They eat the…	flesh
What do zebras and giraffes feed on?	they feed on plants
Where can we find these animals in our country?	in the zoo

In a zoo most animals are kept in…   cages
The lion is sometimes called the…   king of beasts
What do we call animals which are kept at home?   domestic animals/pets

C *Other wild animals*
  1 bear
  2 wolf
  3 hawk
  4 kangaroo
  5 buffalo
  6 camel
  7 ostrich

D Animals drink because they are…   D thirsty
  Before they have had their food animals are…   hungry
  When lions walk up and down in their cage they are…   restless
  To go near a tiger is very…   dangerous
  Some snakes are…   poisonous
  A tortoise walks very…   slowly
  A cheetah runs very…   fast

E *Where do these animals live?*   E
  Lions live…   in the savannah
  Camels live…   in the desert
  Monkeys live…   in the jungle
  Fishes live…   in the water
  Frogs live…   on the land or in the water

F *To which class of animals do they belong?*
Bears are…
Eagles are…
Sharks are…
Snakes are…
Frogs are…
Flies are…

F
mammals
birds
fishes/fish
reptiles
amphibians
insects

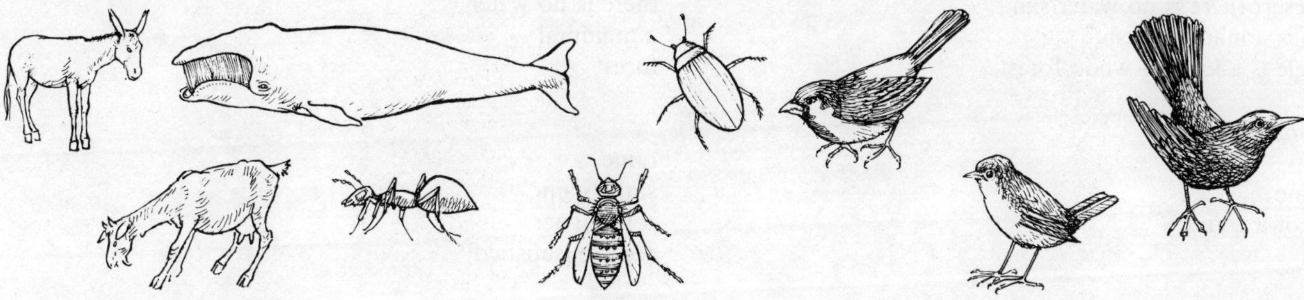

Name three other mammals.
Name three other insects.
Name three other birds.

donkey, goat, whale
wasp, ant, beetle
sparrow, robin, blackbird

G Stanley and Livingstone travelled through the jungle. They were…
People who hunt in an unsportsmanlike or illegal way are called…
What they do is called…
Animals that are hunted are called…
When something is forbidden we can also say that…
Poaching is not allowed means…
Types of animals which don't exist anymore are…
Name an organisation which tries to preserve all sorts of animals.
A trip through the jungle or across the savannah in order to watch or photograph animals is called a…

G
explorers

poachers
poaching
game
it is not allowed
poaching is forbidden
extinct

the World Wildlife Fund

safari

H *Which one is bigger?*
deer/rabbit
elephant/fox
hare/tiger

I *Make your choice:*
We can find the jungle in the tropics/Europe.
In the desert there is no water/sand.
A hippo is a mammal/fish.
The jungle is a kind of wood/forest.

J *Give the opposite of:*
wild
large game
a native of a country
hungry

K *Some proverbs:*
The leopard can not change his spots.
It is the last straw that breaks the camel's back.

H
deer
elephant
tiger

I
in the tropics
there is no water
a mammal
forest

J
tame
small game
a foreigner
replete [satisfied]

K Meanings?

4 Let's go to town

<table>
<tr><td>A</td><td>street</td></tr>
<tr><td></td><td>crossing (junction)</td></tr>
<tr><td></td><td>houses</td></tr>
<tr><td></td><td>shops</td></tr>
<tr><td></td><td>church</td></tr>
<tr><td></td><td>museum</td></tr>
<tr><td></td><td>town-hall</td></tr>
<tr><td></td><td>hotel/restaurant</td></tr>
<tr><td></td><td>theatre</td></tr>
<tr><td></td><td>bank</td></tr>
<tr><td></td><td>bridge</td></tr>
<tr><td></td><td>park</td></tr>
<tr><td></td><td>station</td></tr>
<tr><td></td><td>school building</td></tr>
<tr><td></td><td>traffic-lights</td></tr>
<tr><td></td><td>pedestrians</td></tr>
<tr><td></td><td>zebra-crossing</td></tr>
<tr><td></td><td>bus stop</td></tr>
<tr><td></td><td>street lamp</td></tr>
<tr><td></td><td>pavement</td></tr>
</table>

B	In a town there is a lot of…	B	traffic
	Therefore we say that in a town the traffic is…		heavy
	Pedestrians must walk on the…		pavement
	If possible you must cross the street on a…		zebra-crossing
	If you don't take care when crossing you may…		cause an accident
	When you cross the street without looking you can be…		knocked down by a car
	If you have lost your way you can ask a…		policeman
	What do you ask then?		Officer, please could you tell me the way to Baker Street?

A street where the traffic goes in one direction is a...   one way street
Cars drive on the...   road
Traffic-lights are used to...   regulate the traffic
A green light means: go/cross
A red light means: stop
In England traffic on a roundabout has...   right of way

C *Which word doesn't fit in and why not?*

footpath – avenue – castle	castle. You can't walk on it.
skyscraper – crowd – shop	crowd. It isn't a building.
to walk – to drive – to run	to drive. It isn't done on foot.

D We call the middle of the town the...   town centre
Around the town centre we find the...   suburbs and outskirts
What do we mean by: the surroundings?   the country around the town
A very large city is sometimes called a...   metropolis
The chief city of a country is called the...   capital
Many cities are divided into...   areas or quarters
An important part of every town is the...   shopping-centre
Very narrow streets are called...   alleys
Do you know what slums are?   parts of a city where people live in bad conditions [i.e. in very bad houses]

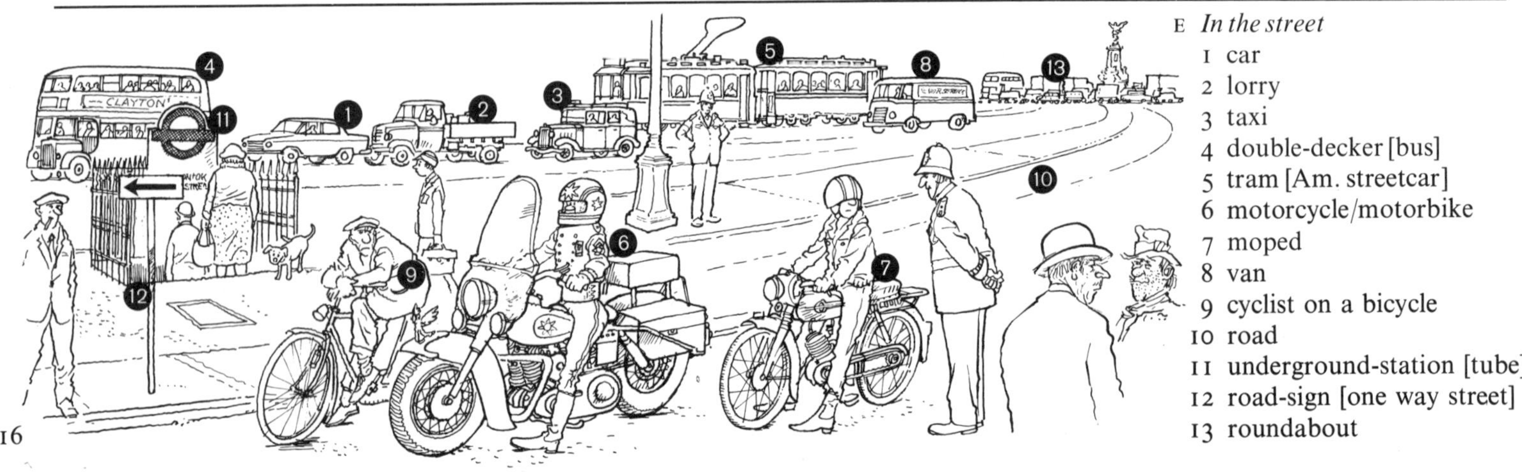

E *In the street*
1 car
2 lorry
3 taxi
4 double-decker [bus]
5 tram [Am. streetcar]
6 motorcycle/motorbike
7 moped
8 van
9 cyclist on a bicycle
10 road
11 underground-station [tube]
12 road-sign [one way street]
13 roundabout

F Buses, trains and cars are...
In London you can also travel...
The underground in London is called the...
During the rush hour

6 a.m. means...
8 p.m. means...
When you want to go by bus you go to a...
When you want to go by train you go to a...
The next bus is due at six means...
Where can you find the time for the arrival of the next train?
When there are many people in each compartment of a train
we say...
BR is short for...
Another word for taxi is...
Buses with two storeys are...
Long-distance buses are called...
Buses are mainly used for...
Coaches travel to...

F means of transport
by underground
tube
many people are going to and from their work
six o'clock in the morning
eight o'clock in the evening
bus-stop or a bus-station
railway-station
the next bus will arrive at six o'clock
on the time-table

the train is crowded
British Rail
cab
double-deckers
coaches
local transport
further destinations

G *Which pairs of words belong together?*
1 pavement   cathedral
2 side-street footpath
3 cab   alley
4 church   taxi
5 town   city

G
1 footpath
2 alley
3 taxi
4 cathedral
5 city

H Name some places where people living in a city can go to for
their amusement.
Name some places where children living in a city can go to
for their recreation.

H
cinema/theatre/music-hall/discotheque/pub/club

playground/sportsground/park/swimming-pool

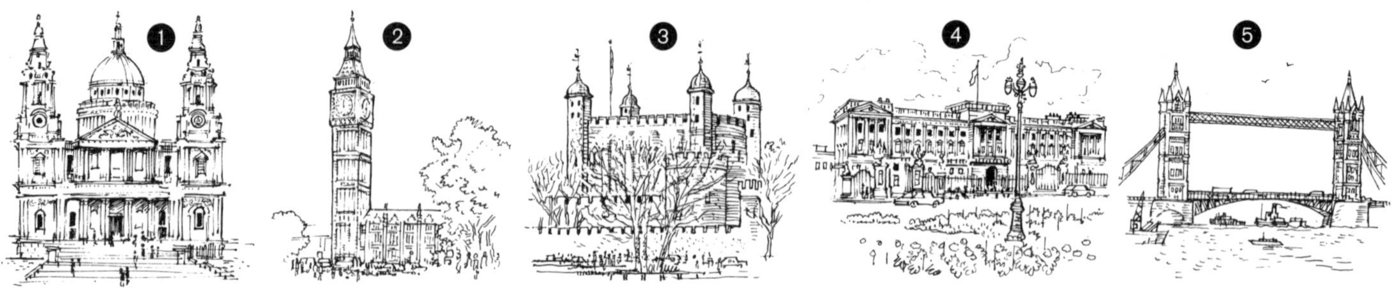

I *Five sights of London. What kind of building is it?*
  1 St. Paul's?
  2 Big Ben?
  3 The Tower of London?
  4 Buckingham Palace?
  5 Tower Bridge?

I
  1 it's a church
  2 it's a tower
  3 it's a castle
  4 it's a palace
  5 it's a bridge

J Children in a city mostly can't play in...
  When they go to school they must be...
  The opposite of careful is...
  In a city many people live in...
  Many shops together form a...
  In a city there are not only houses, flats and shops but also...

J the street
  careful
  careless
  flats [apartment buildings]
  shopping-centre
  offices

K *Give the name of the driver:*
  bus
  taxi
  tram, underground, train
  plane
  car
  bicycle

K
  bus-driver
  taxi-driver
  engine-driver
  pilot
  driver or chauffeur
  cyclist

L *Expressions:*
  God made the country, man made the town. [William Cowper]
  Two is company, three is a crowd.

L Meanings?

5 Going into the countryside

A
1 tent
2 tent-peg
3 tent-pole
4 camper
5 sleeping-bag
6 camp-bed
7 camping chair
8 rucksack
9 pots and pans
10 groundsheet
11 hammock
12 first-aid kit
13 knife
14 axe
15 torch

B Here are some things you need when you go camping. Name them.

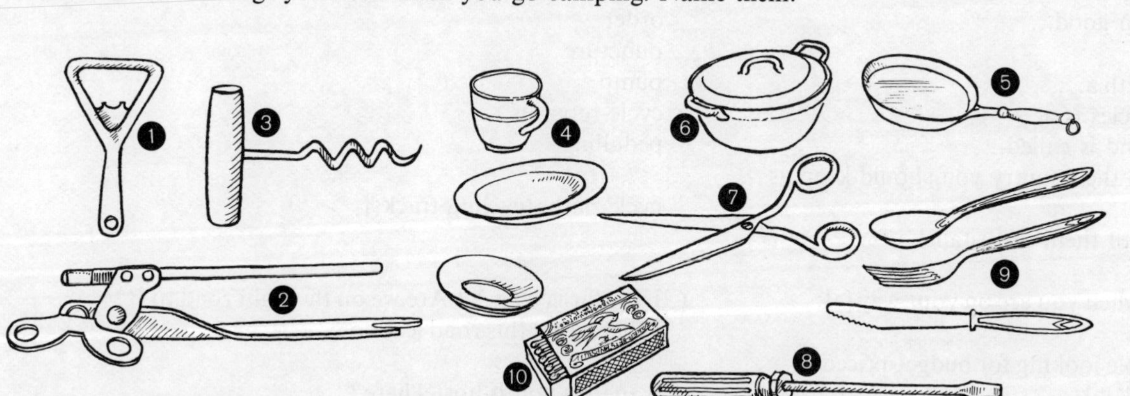

B
1 bottle-opener
2 tin-opener
3 cork-screw
4 crockery [cups, saucers, plates]
5 frying-pan
6 saucepan
7 scissors
8 screwdriver
9 cutlery [forks, knives, spoons]
10 matches

C A place specially meant for camping is a…
For camping on someone's private land you need…
Baths, showers, toilets etc. on a camping-site are called
together the…
The money you have to pay per day is called the…
'Camping prohibited' means…

C camping-site
permission of the owner

sanitary block [toilet]
charge
you are not allowed to camp here

D *Parts of a bicycle*
1 handle-bars
2 bell
3 saddle
4 frame
5 wheel
6 luggage-carrier
7 tyre [tire Am.]
8 chain
9 pedal
10 lamp
11 back-light [rear lamp]
12 dynamo

E The boys want to go for a…
But their bikes are not in good…
One boy has a…
You inflate your tyres with a…
A man who repairs bicycles is a…
Moving the pedals around is called…
When you are cycling in the country you should keep as
much as possible to the…
But there are not many of them in Britain!

E ride on their bikes
order
puncture
pump
cycle-repairer
pedalling

cycle-paths [cycling-tracks]

F Questions you may ask when you are on your way [3]:

Students and young people looking for budget-priced
accommodation often ask [3]:

F How far is it to A? Are we on the right road to B?
Where does this road lead to?

Is there a youth-hostel here?
Is there any inexpensive accommodation near here?
Do you know anyone who can put us up for the night?

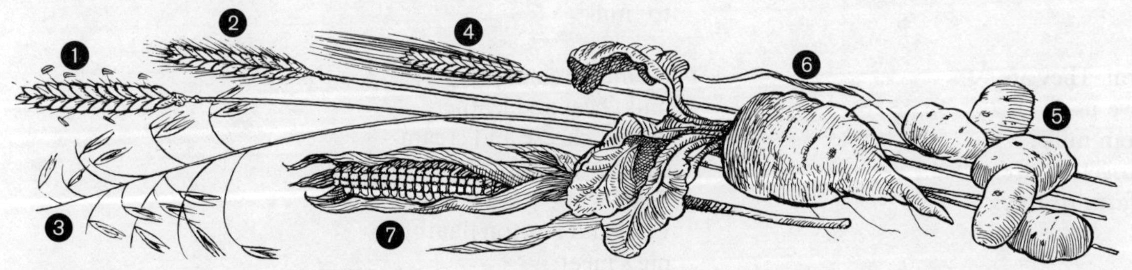

G A road through the fields is called a…
Along the lanes there are sometimes…
The man working in the field is a…
The farmer is sitting on a…
In the middle of the field we see a…
The birds sitting on its shoulders are…
Behind the tractor is a…
What does it cut in the soil?
The farmhand is sowing the…
In the distance we can see a…
On the left is a…

G country-lane
hedges
farmhand
tractor
scarecrow
crows
plough
furrows
seed [grains of corn]
windmill
cart

H The practice of farming is called…
Here are some agricultural products:

H agriculture

1 wheat
2 rye
3 oats
4 barley
5 potatoes
6 sugar-beet
7 maize [Am. corn]

Farmers who keep and raise cattle are engaged in... — cattle farming [dairy farming]
Farmers who grow crops are engaged in... — arable farming
When they do both they practise... — mixed farming

I What do they make from:
wheat... — flour and bread
rye... — bread and cattle food
oats... — porridge and food for animals
barley... — beer and whisky
What do they extract from sugar-beet? — sugar
Wheat, rye, oats and barley together are called... — cereals
The corn is harvested nowadays with a... — combine harvester [combine]
Where does the grass for the cattle grow? — in the fields
Dried grass is called... — hay
Where do the cows graze? — in the meadows
What do cows sleep on in the cowshed? — they sleep on straw

J 'Droppings' of animals we call... — dung/manure
The farmer throws the dung on a... — dung-hill
What is dung used for? — to make the soil fertile
In factories they also make a product which makes the soil
fertile. It's called... — fertilizer

K *Make verbs connected with:*
plough — to plough
seed — to sow – sowed – sown
fertile — to fertilize
food — to feed – fed – fed
milk — to milk

L Mice and rats are not useful. They are... — harmful animals [pests]
Cows are useful. They give us... — milk, beef and leather
What do people make from milk? — butter, cheese and cream
Milk, cheese and butter together are called... — dairy products
The milk goes from the farm to the... — dairy
What do sheep give us? — wool and mutton [lamb]
Pork is... — pig's meat

M Name the buildings and the animals you see on the picture.

M 1 farmhouse
2 stable
3 henhouse
4 kennel
5 horse
6 cow
7 pig
8 sheep
9 goat
10 barn

N *What's the name of the male animal?*

	N
goose	gander
chicken	cock[-erel] [Am. rooster]
horse	stallion
cow	bull
pig	boar
sheep	ram
deer	stag

O *Young animals*

	O
A young cow is called…	a calf
A young horse is called…	a foal
A young sheep is called…	a lamb
A young pig is called…	a piglet

23

 Name the principal forms of the following irregular verbs:
to drive
to eat
to sit
to grow
to ride

drive – drove – driven
eat – ate – eaten
sit – sat – sat
grow – grew – grown
ride – rode – ridden

6 What's your job?

B People doing manual work for wages are called…   B labourers, workers
Bakers, butchers and grocers have shops. They are…   shopkeepers
Carpenters, bricklayers, plumbers etc. are…   tradesmen
They have learned a…   trade
When somebody is an electrician we say…   he is an electrician by trade
When someone is a doctor we say…   he is a doctor by profession

25

Workmen earn…
Wages are paid…
When you are paid monthly it's called…
The general word for wages and salary is…
Most people work because…

wages
weekly
salary
pay
they have to earn a living

C *What do they sell?*
A baker sells…
A butcher sells…
A milkman sells…
A bookseller sells…
A grocer sells…
A greengrocer sells…
A chemist sells…
A tobacconist sells…
When you want to buy pens and paper you go to the…
When you want to buy a gold ring you go to the…
When you want to buy a fresh chicken you go to the…

C

bread and cakes
meat, sausage and chickens
dairy products
books
groceries
fruit and vegetables
toothpaste, cosmetics and soap as well as medicines
tobacco, cigars and cigarettes
stationer's
jeweller's
poulterer's or butcher's

D *Building a house. What are they doing?*
The bricklayer…
The carpenter…
The painter…
The electrician…
The plumber…
The tiler…
The plasterer…
The architect makes the…
When building a house the tradesmen need…
Look at the pictures and name the carpenter's tools. [9]

D

builds the walls
takes care of the woodwork
does the painting
does the wiring
does the plumbing
puts the tiles on the roof
plasters the walls and the ceiling
design for a house
tools
1 hammer
2 pair of pincers
3 chisel
4 drill
5 plane
6 saw
7 yard-stick
8 screwdriver
9 file

E Mr. Johnson is the...
The people working in his office are his...
Mr. Johnson is their...
The lady who makes his appointments is his...
The girls who type his letters are...
The men who take care of the financial administration of
the business are...
The business they all work for is called a...
Sometimes you can find the letters Ltd. after the name of a
company. This is short for...
A smaller office in a different place from the head-office is a...
People to whom the firm or company owes money are...
People who owe money to the firm are...
The boy who does all kinds of jobs is the...
People who have no work are...
We can also say that they have no...
Being out of work means...

E manager of a firm
employees
employer [boss]
secretary
typists

book-keepers
company

Limited [Limited liability company]
branch
creditors
debtors
office-boy
unemployed/jobless
employment/jobs
having no employment

F *At a factory*
Mr. McDonald has a factory. He is a...
People who work in the factory are...
They have been trained to do their jobs so they are...
Another word for factory is...
When a factory makes steel or cotton we call it a...
When a factory produces electricity we call it a...
Another word for work is...
We speak of hard labour when...
All factories together are called...
A town with many factories is an...
A man who works very hard is an...

F manufacturer
factory-hands/workers
skilled workers [workmen]
works
mill
power station [Am. plant]
labour
people are forced to work
industry
industrial town
industrious man

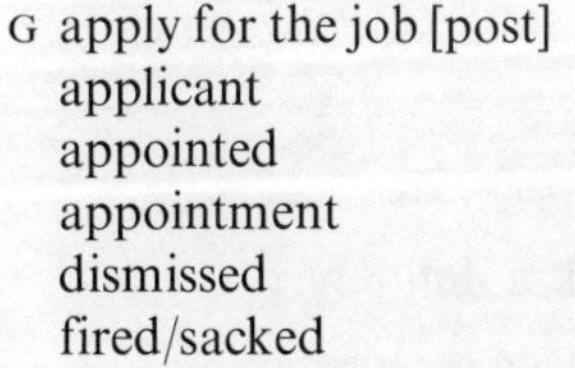

G When there is a vacancy you can...
Then you are an...
When they think you are the right man for the job you are...
So you get the...
When your work is very poor you are...
Other words for 'dismissed' are...

G apply for the job [post]
applicant
appointed
appointment
dismissed
fired/sacked

Sometimes people refuse to work. Then they are... on strike
Most people strike for... better labour-conditions
  or higher wages

Artists sometimes work in a... studio or workshop
What they do or make is called... art

H *Artists*
  1 actor
  2 musician
  3 film star
  4 author
  5 sculptor
  6 playwright
  7 painter
  8 singer

I *Make your choice:*
A draper/hairdresser sells clothes. draper
A barber/merchant sells goods. merchant
A professor/joiner makes furniture. joiner
An optician/potter sells spectacles [glasses]. optician
A tailor/upholsterer makes men's clothes. tailor

J *Give the three principal forms of:*
to choose choose – chose – chosen
to sell sell – sold – sold
to make make – made – made
to strike strike – struck – struck

K *Expressions:* K Meanings?
All work and no play makes Jack a dull boy.
To drive a hard bargain.

28

7 Stop… thief!

A 1 thief
2 telephone box [booth]
3 bag
4 shop window

B The window of the jeweller's shop is…
People who break the law are…
What they do is called…
If the things they have done are not so serious we speak of an…
To know someone when you see him again is to…
Persons who have seen the crime being committed are…
They may be asked to give…
When the police catch the thief he will be taken to the…
There they will put him in a…
But first they will … him.

B smashed
criminals
committing a crime [to commit]

offence
recognize a person
witnesses
evidence
police-station
cell
interrogate

C *At the police-station*
The police will ask the criminal to…
They will also tell him that everything he says will be used…
After the interrogation he will be held in…
Some days or weeks later he has to appear in…

C
make a statement
in evidence against him
custody
court

D *Name the principal forms of the following irregular verbs:*
to bring
to break
to catch
to forgive

D
bring – brought – brought
break – broke – broken
catch – caught – caught
forgive – forgave – forgiven

E *At court*
judge
clerk
the accused
counsel for the prosecution
counsel for the defence
witness
members of the jury
wig
gown

barristers { counsel for the prosecution / counsel for the defence

F A criminal is brought to court for…
He is called the…
He has to stand in the…
The man or woman who pleads for him is his…
The judge may ask:
Then the lawyer answers:
When a lawyer pleads guilty it means that the accused…
The witnesses have to stand in the…
They have to tell the…
They must swear on the…
Then they are…
What the witnesses do is called…
Who have to decide whether the accused is guilty or not?

F trial
accused/defendant
dock
lawyer
what do you plead?
guilty/not guilty
confesses his crime
witness-box
truth
Bible
on oath
testifying
the members of the jury

30

When the jury has decided the judge… — passes the sentence
He has a criminal record means that… — he has been convicted of other crimes
Being sentenced to death is called.. — capital punishment
When somebody is sentenced we can also say that he is… — convicted
Someone who has been convicted is a… — convict

G *Give the opposite of:*

	G
guilty	not guilty [innocent]
just	unjust
legal	illegal
honest	dishonest
to arrest	to release
to confess	to deny

H When you do something which is forbidden by law you… — break the law
Then you should be… — punished
When your offence is not serious you only have to pay some money. This is called a… — fine
When you commit a crime you are… — sent to prison [put in jail]
He was sentenced to six years imprisonment means… — he was sent to prison for six years
In some cases you may only be put on… — probation
When you are on two years probation means that… — you are not punished unless you break the law again within these two years
When you behave well you show… — good conduct

I *Some crimes. What do we mean by:*

	I
theft?	stealing things
kidnapping?	capturing a person and keeping him by force
murder?	killing a person
burglary?	breaking into a house and taking something
robbery?	taking things illegally [often by force]
People who do so are [5]:	thieves/kidnappers/murderers/burglars/robbers

J *Make proverbs from:*

	J
necessity – law	necessity knows no law
poverty – crime	poverty is no crime
one man's meat – poison	one man's meat is another man's poison
honesty – policy	honesty is the best policy

8 In the pub

A public bar
lounge bar
barman
pint of beer
stools
inn sign
cigarette-machine
box of matches
notice 'fully licensed'
dartboard

B Pub is short for…
Over the door outside the pub we mostly find a…
On it is the…
Why do English people go to a pub?

The barman is often a friendly and … man.
He keeps his customers…
The owner of the pub is called the…
At the bar you can buy: [5]
A public house where you can find board and lodgings is
called an…
The owner is the…

B public house
sign
name of the pub
to be in a sociable environment/to drink something/to eat
something/to meet other people
talkative
satisfied
publican
drinks/sandwiches/crisps/nuts/pies

inn [hotel]
inn-keeper [hotel proprietor]

C 1 pint is…
1 litre is…
1 gallon is…

C 0·57 litres
1·76 pints
4·55 litres

D Who's going to buy this round?

I'll get them first. What will it be?

Mine's a pint of mild. Do you want the usual?

Yes, a pint of bitter will do me nicely.

I'm thirsty so I'll have half a pint of lager and lime.

And I'll have a glass of sherry.

Give us a pint of each, please barman, plus half a lager and

lime and a glass of sherry.

Cheers everyone and good health!

E When someone orders a drink for everybody present
he buys a…
When everyone has a drink they all lift their glasses and
say…
If it's someone's birthday you drink to…
In a pub it's often rather…
People are…
In the bar some people play games like:
Someone who drinks continually is an…
He can't stop drinking spirits so he's…
You can also be addicted to…
Such a person is called an…
A person who never drinks alcohol is a…
Someone who's often drunk is a…

E

round

cheers
his/her good health
noisy
chatting and laughing
cards/darts/draughts
alcoholic
addicted to alcohol
drugs, tobacco etc.
addict
teetotaller
drunkard

Name some famous card-games: [4]
All cards together form a...
To give a number of cards to each player is called...
But first the cards must be...

G *A game of chess*
Chess is played on a...
It's played with...
The game is over when one of the kings on the board is [in]...
Here are the chess men:

H *Put it differently:*
He acts as if he's drunk...
It looks as if he's drunk...
I think that he is tipsy...

I *Meals*
Most people have three meals a day viz. [namely]...

When you have a meal late in the evening, this is called...
At four the English have their afternoon-tea with...
When they have their main meal at lunchtime, there is a
lighter meal around six, which is called...

F *Playing cards*
1 ace of clubs
2 king of spades
3 queen of diamonds
4 jack of hearts

poker/bridge/whist/rummy
pack of cards
dealing [to deal]
shuffled [to shuffle]

G

chessboard
chessmen /chess pieces
checkmate

1 king
2 queen
3 bishop
4 knight
5 rook
6 pawn

H

He pretends to be drunk.
He seems to be drunk.
He's tipsy I suppose.

I

breakfast
lunch
dinner [the main meal]
supper
sandwiches, cakes, crumpets etc.

[high]tea

When you get up too late to have breakfast but too early
to have lunch, we say that you are having… brunch
Breakfast time is… early in the morning
Lunchtime is around… midday
12 o'clock in the day time is called… noon
12 o'clock at night is called… midnight

What's the time?
it's half past six
it's a quarter past nine
it's twenty past five
it's twenty-five to ten

a.m. means… before midday [noon] [ante meridiem]
p.m. means… after midday [post meridiem]
most pubs close at… 11 p.m.

J Beer and wine are kept in… J barrels or bottles
Beer from the barrel is called… draught beer
Another type of beer is called… ale
When you're warm, beer and ale are very… refreshing
When you want to open a bottle of wine you must pull out
the… cork
You can do that easily with a… cork-screw

K *Give the principal forms of the underlined irregular verbs:* K
In a pub you always <u>meet</u> a lot of people. meet – met – met
<u>Speak</u> louder I can't hear you because of the noise. speak – spoke – spoken
Joe could not come that night because he <u>was</u> ill. be – was – been
I've never <u>thought</u> about these problems. think – thought – thought

9 At school

A wall
blackboard
chalkbox
desk
teacher
wastepaper basket
floor
ceiling
pupils
school-bag [satchel]
calendar
time-table
map of the United
Kingdom
cupboard

B What schools do you attend when you are:
three years old?
eight years old?
twelve years of age?

B
nursery school
primary school
a secondary school

C What subjects do you study at a secondary school?
Languages…
Mathematics…
Some other subjects are…

C
English, French, German
algebra, geometry
physics / chemistry / biology / history / music /
environmental studies / woodwork / art [drawing] /
needlework / geography / religious studies / cookery

Physics, chemistry and biology together are called…   science
At a grammar school most subjects are…   theoretical subjects
At a technical school most subjects are…   practical subjects
Name some other types of schools with secondary education.   secondary modern school, commercial school

D Where can you find the times for the subjects you are taught?   on the time-table
Where is the blackboard?   in front of the classroom
Where can we find the map of the United Kingdom?   on the wall
Where can you find the days of the week?   on the calendar
Name the days of the week.   Sunday, Monday, Tuesday, Wednesday, Thursday, Friday, Saturday
Name the months of the year.   January, February, March, April, May, June, July, August, September, October, November, December
A schoolyear is divided into three…   terms
These are…   the autumn term, the spring term, the summer term
When you have a few days off you have a…   holiday
Large schools with different types of education are…   comprehensive schools
Another type of school for children from 8–13 years old is the…   middle school

E *English and American educational systems*
English
under 3…   play school
3 till 5…   nursery school
5 till 7…   infant school } primary school
7 till 11…   junior school }
11 till 16 or older…   secondary school
university [college]

American
under 6…   nursery school
6 till 11 [grade 1–6]…   elementary school
12 till 14 [grade 7–9]…   junior high [school]
15 till 18 [grade 10–12]…   senior high [school]
over 18…   college or university

F Name several things you can write with.   F pen and ink / ballpoint [biro] / pencil / fountain pen / chalk / crayons

G Arithmetic means...
How do you say in words:
2 × 6 =
3 + 5 =
7 − 1 =
8 ÷ 4 =
  × means ...
  + means ...
  − means ...
  ÷ means ...
0.47 is...

G doing sums

two times six is [equals]
three and five makes [is]
seven minus one equals [is]
eight divided by four is [equals]
to multiply
to add
to subtract
to divide
a decimal fraction

H *Reading and writing*
What can you read?
Many books are divided up into...
Every page has a number. We say...
On this page there are a great number of...
The words form...
At the end of a sentence you find a...
Sentences form together a...
A part of a text is called a...
The space on the left side of the page is the...

H

letters, books, magazines, comics, newspapers
chapters
the pages are numbered
words
sentences
full stop
text
paragraph
margin

What do you call them?
, ...
? ...
! ...
[] ...

a comma
a question mark
an exclamation mark
brackets

I When you go to the primary school for the first time,
you go into the...
When you go to a secondary school for the first time,
you go into the...
What happens at nine o'clock in the morning?
Who teaches you English?
When all your work is correct you get...
For poor work you get...

I

first class

first form
school begins
your English teacher
full marks
low marks

When you are in the last form of a secondary school you
have to take an…

exam[ination]

When you go in for an exam you can do the subjects on
different…

levels viz. O-level or A-level

What do the 'O' and 'A' stand for in O-level and A-level?

Ordinary and Advanced

J 1 school building
   2 playground
   3 entrance
   4 headmaster
   5 bicycle-shed

K *Give the opposite of:*
a clever boy
poor work
full marks
to pass [an exam]
the written exam
the examiner

K
a stupid boy
good work
low marks
to fail
the oral exam
the candidate

L *Give the comparative of the underlined word:*
a <u>good</u> pupil
a <u>bad</u> pupil
a <u>difficult</u> examination

L
a better pupil
a worse pupil
a more difficult examination

M *Make nouns from:*
    to examine
    to multiply
    to add [up]
    to subtract
    to divide
    to teach [taught – taught]

M
    examination, examiner
    multiplication
    addition
    subtraction
    division
    teacher

N *Make your choice:*
    Doing sums is called reading/arithmetic.
    You can find the meaning of a word in your satchel/the dictionary.
    On the time-table you can find the days of the week/the subjects you are taught.
    Changing a word from English into Dutch is called subtraction/translating

N
    arithmetic

    the dictionary

    the subjects you are taught

    translating

O *Expressions*
    Never put off till tomorrow what you can do today.
    Learn this lesson by heart. [meaning?]

10 What's on tonight?

A 'What's on tonight' can mean:

	A what radio programme
	what T.V. programme
	what film
	what play
	what floorshow
	what concert

is there tonight?

All things mentioned above are called…   entertainment
The man whose work it is to amuse people who attend a
show is an…   entertainer
The people in the theatre are the…   audience

B Programmes on radio and T.V. are…   B broadcasts
BBC means…   British Broadcasting Corporation
Sometimes a broadcast is interrupted by a…   newsflash [something very important has happened]
There are three T.V. [television] channels/stations in Britain
viz. [namely]…   BBC 1
                                                         BBC 2
                                                         ITV [Independent T.V. It's commercial]

We are given information about programmes by the…
The programmes are broadcast from the…
We can receive the programmes through a…
To send a programme by radio or T.V. is called…
When there is something wrong with the reception of
programmes we say…
Radios and T.V. sets are…
A radio is sometimes called a…

announcer
studios of a radio or T.V. station
T.V. set
transmitting

there is some interference on our set
receivers [of programmes]
wireless

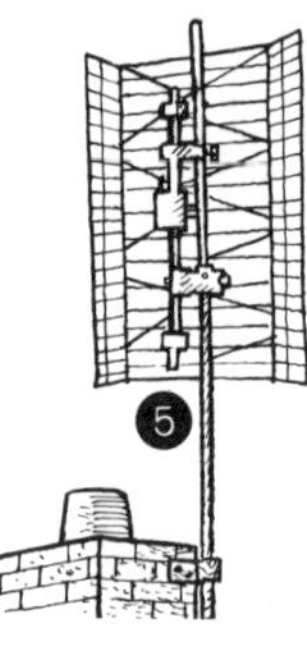

C *T.V. set*
1 volume
2 contrast
3 on/off switch
4 channel switches
5 aerial
6 screen

D *At the cinema*
At the cinema we can see a…
Some types of films are [6]…

D
film
a slapstick film / a thriller / a cartoon [animated film] /
a Western / a horror picture / a documentary film

The man who makes a film is the…
A well-known actor in a film is a…
Apart from the feature film we can also see the… at a
cinema.

producer
film star/movie star
newsreel and some advertisements

Between two films there is an...   interval [intermission Am.]
You know what people in a foreign film say because of the...   subtitles
In some cinemas the programme goes on all day. Then we speak of a...   continuous performance
On Saturday nights there are often...   late night showings
If you want to be sure of getting a seat it is best to...   book in advance

E   *Give the principal forms of:*

to go   go – went – gone
to stand   stand – stood – stood
to understand   understand – understood – understood
to write   write – wrote – written

F   *At the theatre*

When you want to see a play you go to the...   theatre
The people in the play are the...   actors/actresses
What they do is called...   acting
The showing of the play is the...   performance
The parts of the play are the...   acts
Each act may consist of several...   scenes
The plays are being performed on the...   stage
The background on the stage is the...   scenery
The man who sees to it that everything on the stage is in order is the...   stage-manager
The seats downstairs are the...   stalls
The seats upstairs are the...   circle/balcony
All actors who act the parts of the play are called together the...   cast
Before the play is ready to be performed the actors must practise their parts in...   rehearsals
The final rehearsal is the...   dress-rehearsal
What's the first show called?   the première
An afternoon performance is a...   matinée
When you enter the theatre you can put your coats in the...   cloakroom

G Where can you find details about the play and the actors?
When people think it a good play they clap their hands to
show their…
Clapping our hands is called…
The man who has written the play is the…
Kinds of plays:[3]

G in the programme you can buy

appreciation
applauding
playwright
a comedy
a tragedy
a musical

H *Give the female word connected with:*
actor
waiter
author
ballet dancer

H

actress
waitress
authoress
ballet dancer [male and female]

I Where do you go if you want to:
dance? [3]

see a film?
listen to an opera? [2]

see a floorshow or cabaret?

I

to a disco[theque]
to a ballroom
to a dance hall
to a cinema
to a concert hall
to an opera house
to a night-club

J *Saying*
All the world's a stage
and all the men and women merely players.
[William Shakespeare]

11 My home is my castle

A 1 bungalow
2 cottage
3 mansion
4 block of flats
   [apartment-building, Am.]
5 detached houses
6 terraced houses

The roof of the cottage in the picture is a…	thatched roof
It is covered with…	thatch [reeds]
The roof of the bungalow is a…	tiled roof
A block of flats consists of a number of…	apartments/flats

B When you want to buy a house you look for houses with a
notice: …

B

house for sale

You can buy a house through an…
estate-agent

If you don't have enough money you can borrow it from a... bank or building society
Then you take a... mortgage
Of course you have to pay... interest
And the money you have borrowed has to be... repaid
The opposite of 'to borrow from' is... to lend to
The person who deals with the legal side of buying a house
is a... solicitor
The man who designs the house is the... architect
When you own a house you have to pay a local tax on
property called... rates
These taxes are used on: ... education, roads and other public services

C If you live in a house which is not yours you have to pay... C rent
The man who receives the rent is your... landlord
The man or woman who rents the house is the... tenant
Council houses are houses built by the... local authorities
[municipal council]

D *Building a house*
Name the parts of the house:

1 roof
2 window
3 wall
4 chimney
5 gutter
6 foundations
7 fence
8 garden

The roof of the house is... a sloping roof
The roof of a house can also be... flat

E Wood prepared for building is called... E timber
The strips of wood used for the floors are... boards
We call the beams of the roofs... rafters

46

Name some materials houses can be built of: [4]
The man who builds the house is the...
When there are more people concerned we speak of a...

bricks/stone/concrete/wood
builder/contractor
building company

F Around the house we find the...
Around the garden we sometimes find a...
In the fence there is a...
The man who takes care of the garden is the...
Some of his jobs are: [4]

F garden
fence
gate
gardener
mowing the lawn, weeding the flowerbeds, planting flowers,
growing vegetables

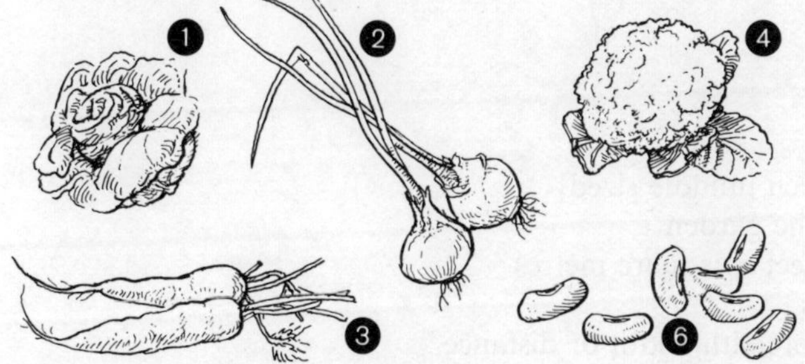
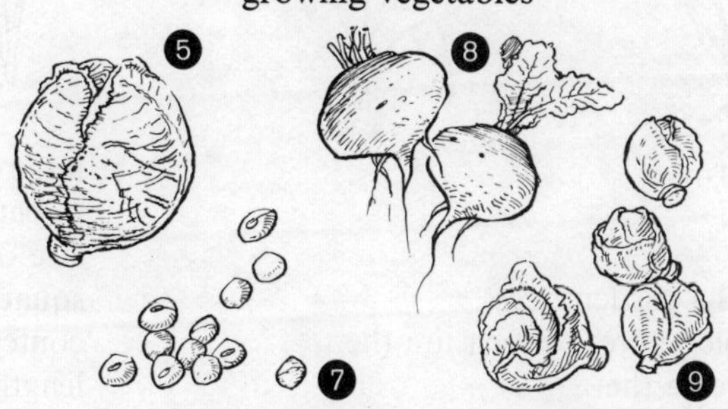

Some vegetables
1 lettuce
2 onions
3 carrots
4 cauliflower
5 cabbage
6 beans
7 peas
8 turnips
9 brussels sprouts

G Flowers grow in: [3]

Those grown in greenhouses and gardens are...
The flowers in the fields are...
Here are some wild flowers: [5]

G flowerbeds
greenhouses
the fields
cultivated flowers
wild flowers

1 daisy
2 poppy
3 lily of the valley
4 buttercup
5 dandelion

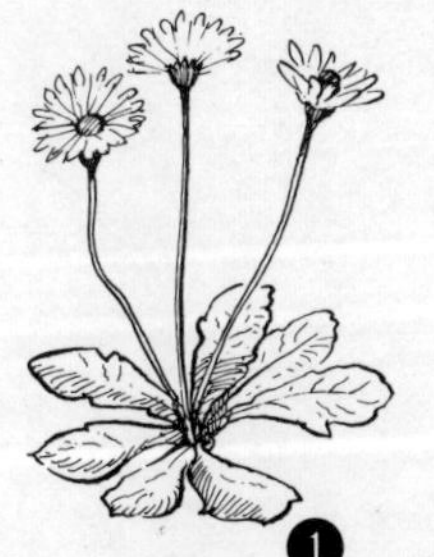
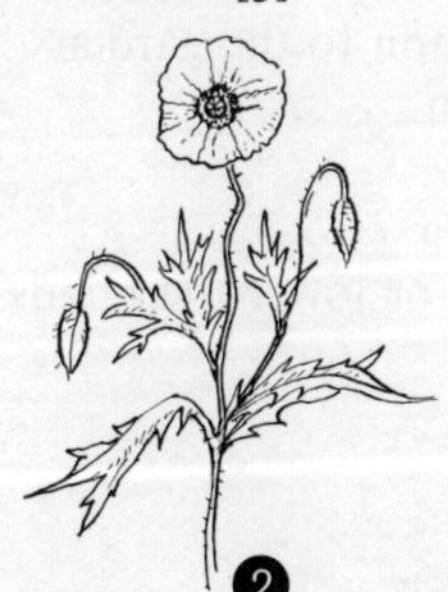
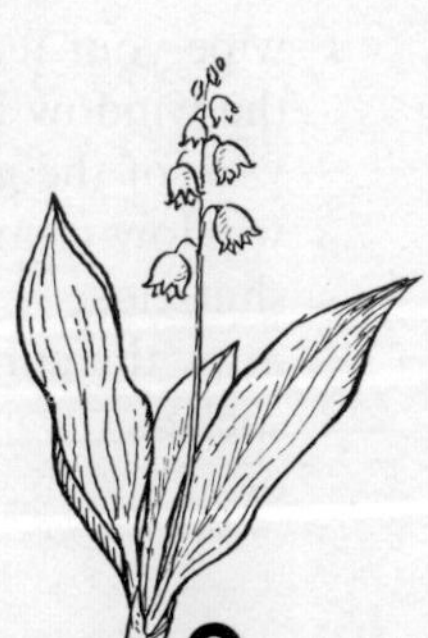

Here are some cultivated flowers [5]:

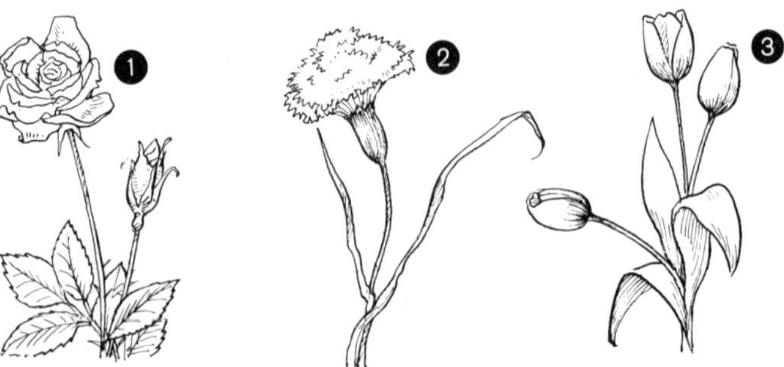
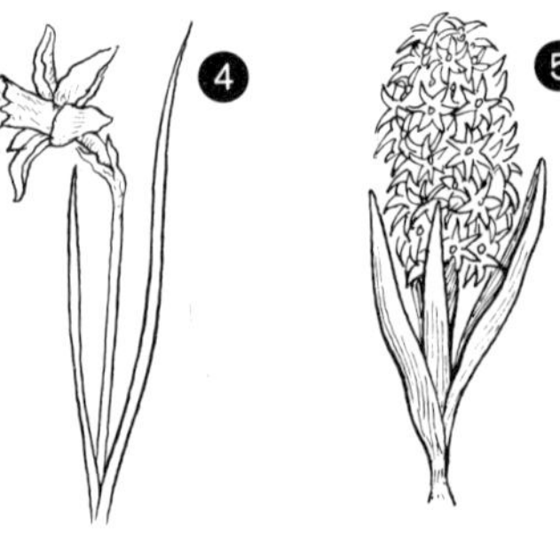

H A garden can be small or…
Or just…
We call that the…
We measure the size of the garden in…
We use cubic feet or cubic metres to measure the…
We use the 'mile' to indicate the…

H large
in between [middle sized]
size of the garden
square feet or square metres
contents
length, breadth/width or distance

I *Make adjectives from:*
length
breadth
width
depth

I
long
broad
wide
deep

J Before entering a house you should…
When you can see the garden from the window we say…
From the window you then have a…
The man whose job it is to clean the windows is the…
When it's cold we … the windows.
And in the evening we…
We pull the plugs out of the…
And we switch [turn] the lights…

J wipe your feet [shoes] on the doormat
the window looks on to the garden
view of the garden
window-cleaner
shut/close
draw the curtains or lower the blinds
sockets
off

48

12 What's your favourite sport?

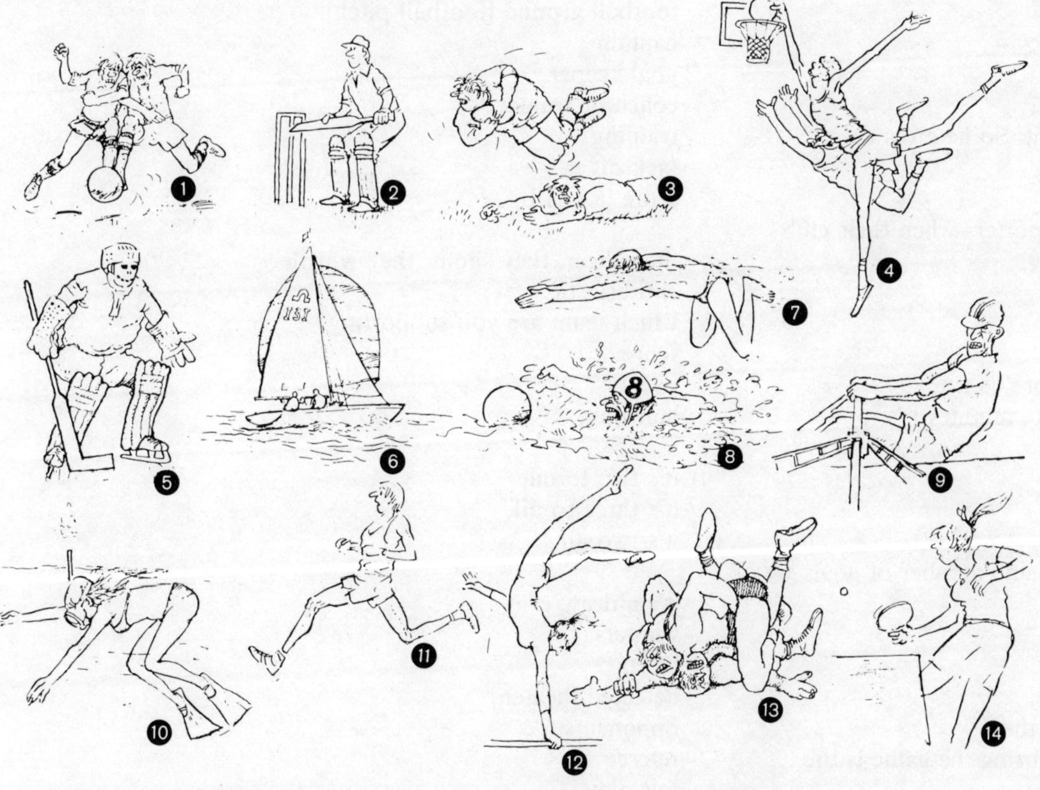

A 1 football [soccer]
   2 cricket
   3 rugby
   4 basketball
   5 ice-hockey
   6 sailing
   7 swimming
   8 water-polo
   9 rowing
  10 skin-diving
  11 athletics
  12 gymnastics
  13 wrestling
  14 table-tennis

B *Groups of sports*

1–5 are…

The opposite of a team sport is an…

We can also divide the sports into: [2]

B

team sports

individual sport

indoor sports

outdoor sports

49

C *Football* [*soccer*]

Someone who plays in a team is a…	player
When you play in a football team you are a…	football player [footballer]
The games take place on the…	football ground [football pitch]
The leader of the team is the…	captain
The man in the goal is the…	goal-keeper
The instructor of the team is the…	coach or trainer
It's his work to keep the players fit. So he gives them…	training
The beginning of a match is the…	kick-off
Each team tries to…	score [a goal]
What are the reactions of the supporters when their club has scored?	they cheer, they shout, they whistle
They are very…	enthusiastic
Whose side are you on means…	which team are you supporting?
The result of the match is the…	score
Another meaning of the word 'score' is…	twenty
When the teams have played for 45 minutes it's…	half-time

D

It's 2–1 means…	it's two to one
It's 3–0 means…	it's three to nil
It's 2–2 means…	it's two all
When the teams have scored the same number of goals we say…	it's a draw
If a team wins they are called the…	winners
If it loses the match they are the…	losers
The losers were … by the winners.	defeated [beaten]
The players of the other team are the…	opponents
The man who enforces the rules during the game is the…	referee
Playing correctly is called…	fair play
Incorrect play is called…	foul play
When a player breaks the rules the other team may get a [2]…	free kick, penalty kick
Sometimes an offender gets a[n] [2]…	[official] warning, yellow card
A paid player is a…	professional
One who only plays for the love of the game is an…	amateur
Rugby is sometimes called…	rugger
A federation of football clubs is a…	[football] league

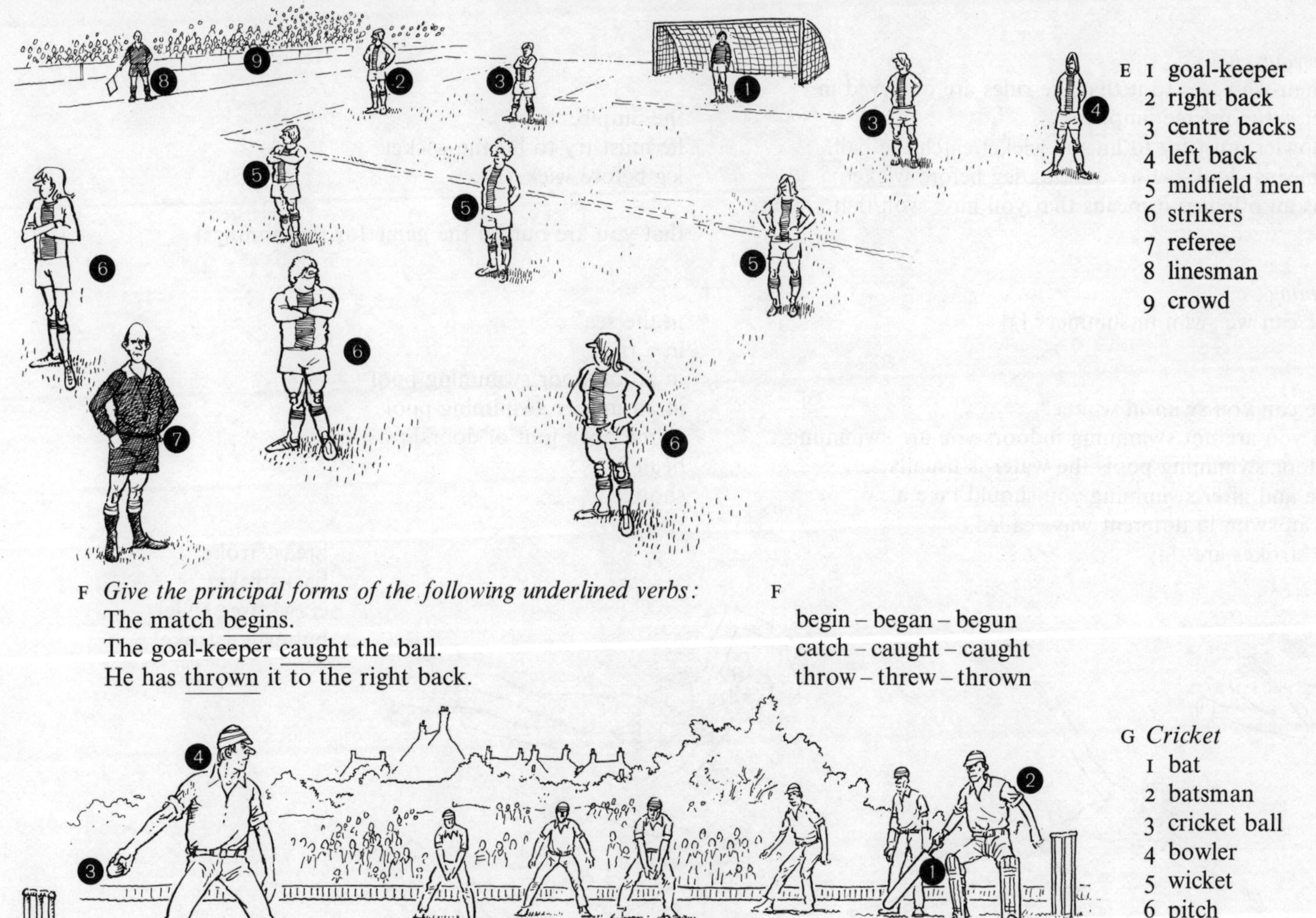

F *Give the principal forms of the following underlined verbs:*
The match begins.
The goal-keeper caught the ball.
He has thrown it to the right back.

begin – began – begun
catch – caught – caught
throw – threw – thrown

H *Make your choice:*
The man who sees to it that the rules are observed in
cricket is the referee/umpire.
The bowler must try to hit the wicket/catch the ball.
Lbw means: look before walking/leg before wicket.
Lbw is an offence; it means that you have won/that you are
out.

the umpire
he must try to hit the wicket
leg before wicket

that you are out [of the game for that innings]

I *Swimming*
Where can we swim in summer? [3]

in the sea
in a river
in an outdoor swimming pool
in an indoor swimming pool
in the open [out of doors]

Where can you swim in winter?
When you are not swimming indoors you are swimming…
In indoor swimming pools the water is usually…
Before and after swimming you should take a…
You can swim in different ways called…
These strokes are: [4]

heated
shower
strokes

breaststroke
backstroke
crawl [free style]
butterfly [stroke]

When you plunge into the water with your head down and
your arms stretched forward you…
When you do so you are a…
A team sport played in the water is…

dive
diver
water-polo

J *Athletics*

An open air arena for athletics is a… stadium
The people who watch the games are the… spectators/crowd
The place for the spectators is… on the stand or the grand-stand
Important athletic games are the… Olympic Games
They are held… every four years
A good loser is called a… good sport
Some athletic sports are: jumping [high-jump, long-jump, pole-vault]
running/hurdling/throwing the javelin

K A volleyball game starts with the… K serve
What kind of a sport is volleyball? a team sport
The man who comments on a match on radio or T.V. is a… reporter/commentator

L *Some more sports are:*

L 1 boxing
2 riding
3 skating
4 racing

13 A day at the races

A 1 race-horse
2 jockey
3 race-track
4 finish
5 bookmaker

B *Look at the picture.*
Tell about the order of arrival.
Number 16 comes…
Number 19 comes…
Number 3 comes…
Number 22 comes…

C A man or woman riding a race-horse is a…
When you are riding a horse you are…
When you want to bet on a horse you go to a…
Number 12 pays 8–1 means…

Put it differently:
Almost everybody thinks no. 16 will win…
Hardly anybody thinks no. 19 will win…

B

first
last
second
third

C jockey
on horseback
bookmaker or the tote
if you lay a bet on no. 12 and it wins you get back 8 times
as much money

no. 16 is the favourite
no. 19 is an outsider

When two horses almost finish together, so that it's
difficult to see who has won, we speak of a…   close finish
When a photo has to be used to determine the winner it's
called a…   photo-finish
After the race you can see the results on the…   board
The next day you can also read them in the…   newspapers
When a horse has done its best it may get a reward in the
form of a…   lump of sugar

D *Name the principal forms of:*

D

to win   win – won – won
to lose   lose – lost – lost
to run   run – ran – run

E *Name three racing sports:*

E

horse-racing
motorcycle-racing
motor-racing
car-racing

When you run a race in less time than anyone else before,
you…   set up a new record
Perhaps even a…   world record
Then you are the…   champ[ion]
So the most important thing in racing is…   speed
Racing mostly takes place on a…   circuit or race-track
As motor-racing is very expensive most drivers are being…   sponsored
This means that they receive…   money from a person or firm so that they can race
The race is over when the competitors pass the…   finishing line
From start to finish means…   from the beginning to the end
He who wins gets the…   first prize

55

G *Riding*
1 horseman/rider
2 saddle
3 stirrup
4 riding-boots
5 reins
6 bridle
7 riding-crop
8 harness
9 pack of hounds

When a horse runs fast it...
When it doesn't go so fast it...
The reins are used for...
Horses are used in sport for: [4]

gallops [to gallop]
trots [to trot]
guiding a horse
show-jumping/horse-racing/fox-hunting/cross-country racing

H *Give the opposite of:*
   to win
   to start
   to speed up
   relatively

H
   to lose
   to finish
   to slow down
   absolutely

14 A pop concert

B What kind of music does a pop group play?
  Pop is short for…
  What's the name of the group in the picture?
  Another word for a group of musicians is a…
  People who make music are…
  The man who sings is the…
  A song which is a great success is a…

B pop music, rock 'n roll
  popular
  Rebound
  band
  musicians
  singer
  hit

C Young people under twenty are…
The growing up period is called…
When you are around fifty you are…
What would you call a man who is over sixty-five?

C teenagers
adolescence
middle-aged
an old-age pensioner [senior citizen]

D Name the musical instruments in the picture.
Give the names of the people who play these instruments.

D
drums – drummer
guitar – guitarist
organ – organist
piano – pianist

E *Give the principal forms of:*
to sing
to show
to leave

E
sing – sang – sung
show – showed – shown
leave – left – left

F *Some more musical instruments*

F 1 flute
2 saxophone
3 violin
4 harp
5 trumpet
6 tuba
7 trombone
8 recorder
9 tambourine
10 xylophone
11 cello

G These instruments are used in an…
　The man who conducts the orchestra is the…
　The man who leads a band is a…
　What kind of music is often played by an orchestra?
　Some other kinds of music are:

G orchestra
　conductor
　leader
　classical music
　rhythm and blues, jazz, soul, folkmusic

Here is an old English folksong:

H A pop group mostly plays in a…
　A place where teenagers go dancing is a…
　What's a pop festival?

H concert hall or disco[theque]
　disco
　an open air pop concert where a number of groups play

I *What do they do?*
　A disc-jockey…
　A musician…
　A singer…
　A road-manager [roady]…

I
　plays records in discotheques or on the radio
　plays music
　sings a song
　takes care of the equipment of the group

J A machine on which you can play records is a…
　Teenagers like to play…
　A small record is called a…
　A large record is called a…
　You can buy records at a…
　Records are kept in…
　A long-playing record of a pop group is an…
　Records are recorded in a…
　In a pub records are played on a…

J record-player
　records/discs
　single
　long-playing record [LP]
　record-shop
　sleeves
　album
　recording-studio
　juke-box

An LP is played at...   33 revolutions per minute [33 r.p.m.]

K *Give the opposite of:*
a single
loud, noisy
classical music
instrumental music

K
a long-playing record
quiet
modern music
vocal music

L *Elements of a pop song*
Give one or more words for:
the rhythm of the music
the words of the song
the melody of the song
the speed of the music

L
the beat
the text, the lyrics
the tune
the tempo

M *What sounds do the animals make?*
horses...
pigs...
cocks...
hens...
dogs...
pigeons...
cows...
sheep...
ducks...
frogs...
birds...
bees...

M
neigh
grunt
crow
cackle
bark
coo
low
bleat
quack
croak
twitter
hum

15 Casting your vote

A Britain is ruled by the people. It is therefore called a...
The group of people who rule a country is the...
What they do is called...
The people elect [=choose] a man or woman to represent them in Parliament. He or she is their...
An MP represents the people of a certain district. This district is called a...
Parliament consists of...
In the House of Commons are the...
In the House of Lords are...
The chairman of the House of Commons is the...
The chairman of the House of Lords is the...
Who also play an important part in governing the country?
All ministers together are called...
A minister is the head of a...
A man who is in 'rank' just below a minister is called a...
Some important departments are: [3]

The head of the Cabinet is the...
Some other ministers are: [5]

A democracy
government
governing

MP [Member of Parliament]

constituency
the House of Commons and the House of Lords
MP's
Peers and bishops
Speaker
Lord Chancellor
the ministers
the Cabinet
ministry [=department]
junior minister
the Home Office
the Foreign Office
the Treasury
Prime Minister
the Minister of Education
the Chancellor of the Exchequer
the Home Secretary
the Foreign Secretary
the Minister of Defence

B The basic law of a country is called the...
When a political group wants a new law they...
The bill must be passed by both...
Then it becomes an...
If one of the Houses has an objection the bill is...
The act becomes a law as soon as...

B constitution [in United Kingdom: Common Law]
introduce a bill
Houses
act [of Parliament]
rejected [to reject]
the Queen has signed it

C On the poster you can see that today there is a...
So today is...
This building is a...
Here you must...
You put your ballot in the...
Then you are a...
You vote for a...
A secret ballot means that...
The main political parties in Britain are: [3]

When you come of age [18] you have the right to vote. This is called...
Put differently: to come of age.
When you have full rights in a country you are a...

C general election
election day
polling-station
cast your vote
ballot-box
voter
representative of your political party
nobody knows to whom you give your vote
the Labour party
the Conservative party
the Liberal party

suffrage
to reach the age of majority
citizen of that country

D *Make your choice:*
Someone concerned with politics is a policeman/politician
Another word for county is province/shire
To unite means to bring together/to set apart
The opposite of 'to unite' is: to reign/to separate
An embassy/ambassador is the representative of his native
country in a foreign country.

D
politician
shire
to bring together
to separate

ambassador

E England, Scotland, Wales and Northern Ireland together
are called the...
In the past Britain had a lot of...
Nowadays most colonies have...
That means that...
People who are the property of others are...
More than a century ago there was ... in most colonies.
But now slavery has been...

E

United Kingdom
colonies
home rule
they have a government of their own/are independent
slaves
slavery
abolished

F *Give the principal forms of the underlined verbs:*
to cast one's vote
to come of age
to hold an election
he may win the elections

F

cast – cast – cast
come – came – come
hold – held – held
may – might

G *Local authorities*
The local authorities rule over a...
The head of a municipality is the...
In London this man is called the...
The ruling body of a municipality is the...
People chosen from and by the council to assist the mayor
are...

G

municipality [=town or district]
mayor
Lord Mayor
town-council or municipal council

aldermen

16 At church

A
1 bride
2 bridegroom
3 bridesmaid
4 entrance
5 church-tower
6 church-bells
7 weather-cock
8 stained glass window
9 churchyard
10 [small] steeple

B This ceremony is called a…
The bride and bridegroom have just been…
This day is their…
They look very…
From now on they are … and …
Before they were married they were…
When you are engaged you can say: he [she] is my…
The first weeks of a marriage are called the…
Name other words with 'wedding': [4]

B wedding
married [to marry]
wedding-day
happy
husband and wife
engaged
fiancé[e]
honeymoon
wedding-ring
wedding-cake
a golden wedding
a silver wedding

C Among the wedding guests are the couple's...
The sister of your father or mother is your...
The brother of your father or mother is your...
What's the son or daughter of your aunt called?
Your brother's or sister's son is your...
Their daughter is your...
The oldest man in the picture is probably...
Who's the oldest woman in the picture?
When you are not married you are...
A man who is not married is called a...
A woman who's not married is sometimes called a...

C relatives
aunt
uncle
your cousin
nephew
niece
grandfather
grandmother
single
bachelor
spinster

D The official church in England is...
Who's the head of the Roman Catholic church?
He lives in the...
Who's the founder of the Mohammedan religion?
The highest officials in the Church of England are...
Other clergymen in the Church of England are...

D the Anglican Church [Church of England]
the Pope
Vatican
the prophet Mohammed
archbishops and bishops
deans
vicars
rectors

A district in the care of a rector or vicar is a...
A bishop is the head of a...
The man who looks after the church-building is the...

parish
diocese
sexton/verger

E 1 cathedral
2 mosque
3 synagogue
4 chapel

 The people who attend services in a synagogue are...

Jewish people

G A church is a place of…	G worship
In church you sing…	psalms or hymns
The vicar says a…	prayer [to pray]
The vicar gives the…	sermon
At the end of the service the vicar gives the congregation his…	blessing

H You usually go to church to attend a…	H service
In the Roman Catholic church the service is called…	mass
When you have a religion you believe in…	God
Another word for religion [less common] is…	creed
When something is very difficult to believe we say it's almost…	incredible
We find God's word in the…	Bible
We can divide the Bible into two large parts:	the Old Testament the New Testament

The first book of the Old Testament tells us about the...   creation
Adam and Eve lived in...   paradise
The first four books of the New Testament are called the...   gospels
The first one is the...   gospel according to St. Matthew
Jesus Christ died on the...   Cross [he was crucified]
God's opponent is the...   Devil [the Evil One]
The bad things we do are called our...   sins

I *What do they live in?*   I

A monk...   lives in a monastery
A nun...   lives in a convent/nunnery
A vicar...   lives in a vicarage
A parson...   lives in a parsonage
A rector...   lives in a rectory

J A priest is addressed as...   J father [followed by his family name]
Another word for family name is...   surname
To christen a child means...   to give it a name before God
This name is his [her]...   christian name [first name]
The ceremony of sprinkling a small child with water from
the font in church is called...   baptism [to baptize]

K *Give the opposite of:*   K
hell   heaven
happy   sad/unhappy

L *Make your choice:*
He is a religion/religious man.
To confess/to believe means to tell one's sins.
To do/to make a confession.
God created the world means God made the world/God
punished the world.
Someone who has become a believer is a convict/convert.

M

L
religious man
to confess
to make a confession

God made the world
a convert [to convert]

M 1 saint
2 angel
3 ghost [spirit]

17 At a fashion-parade

A 1 We'll first show you clothes worn on the beach. These
clothes are called…
The lady is wearing a…
And on her head she has a…
The opposite of summer-wear is…
The young man is wearing a dark coloured pair of…
Say differently: They are not too expensive.

2 Our next section concerns…
First we see Carol in…
Are the pyjamas too tight? No, they're…
Below the knees the trouser-legs are…

A

beach-wear
spotted and striped bikini
flowered swimming-cap
winter-wear
swimming-trunks
they are reasonably priced

night-wear
a pair of pyjamas
slim-fitting
flared

How is her jacket fastened? It's… buttoned down the front
Around the neck and wrists there is… a collar and cuffs
The pants and top go well together. They are… matching
Next is Jane. Jane is wearing a… long flowing nightdress
The front of the nightdress is… embroidered
Thank you.

3 This is Barbara. She's wearing an… evening-dress
It is worn outside with a… fur cape
Silk and satin are not 'in' this year means that these
materials are not… suitable for this year's fashion
Barbara's clothes are always up to date, in other words: … Barbara is always dressed in the latest fashion
Name some of her pieces of jewellery: [4] a bracelet/earrings/a necklace/a brooch
Name some precious metals: [3] gold/silver/platinum
Some precious stones are: [3] ruby/emerald/diamond
You see a lot of skirts and blouses this year. This means
that they are… in fashion
Daniel is wearing a three-piece… evening-suit
Around his neck he is wearing a… bowtie

4 What do we call the sort of clothes you see in picture 4? casual wear
The gentleman is wearing smart… trousers and a tweed jacket
And over his arm he has a… waterproof raincoat [mac]
The lady on his left is dressed in a… safari-suit
On her head she has a wide-brimmed… hat
She has her hands in the … of her jacket. pockets
Around the waist she wears a… belt

5 Here we have some youngsters in… jeans and jumpers
These clothes are for… everyday wear
What kind of shirt is one boy wearing? a T-shirt

6 Outsize clothes are… clothes for people who need larger sizes
Clothes for mothers-to-be are called… maternity-wear
Put differently: We have a large number of different
clothes. we have a good selection of clothes

Dark shades of colour make you look…
Materials can be striped in various ways. Name them. [3]

Another word for clothes is…

B *This is your size*
Women only. dresses/suits

American	10	12	14	16	18	20
British	32	34	36	38	40	42

Men only. suits/overcoats

American }						
British }	36	38	40	42	44	46

C Patterns for materials have to be…
The person who draws designs is a…
The new collection of clothes is shown by…
Mannequins are…
Here are some materials clothes can be made of: [5]
Some more materials are: [6]
Materials mostly have different…
Name some patterns: [4]
When the material has no pattern we speak of…

slimmer
horizontally
vertically
diagonally
garments

C designed
designer
mannequins
professional models
nylon/cotton/wool/velvet/linen
corduroy/lace/leather/flannel/denim/suede
patterns
striped/spotted/checked/flowered
plain material

D *Give the principal forms of the underlined irregular verbs.*
He <u>spends</u> much money on clothes.
I've just <u>read</u> a fashion magazine.
Did you <u>see</u> the fashion show last week?
To <u>blow</u> your nose you need a hanky [handkerchief].

D
to spend – spent – spent
to read – read – read
to see – saw – seen
to blow – blew – blown

E The opposite of 'in fashion' is…
A model must be beautiful so she [he] sometimes has
to go to a…
A person skilled in the use of cosmetics is a…
The treatment of fingers, hands and nails is called…
A woman doing this professionally is a…
What's the treatment of feet called?

E out of fashion

beauty-parlour
beautician
manicure
manicurist
chiropody

F
1 bath
2 bathroom cabinet
3 bath-salts
4 deodorant
5 face-cloth/flannel
6 towel
7 talcum-powder
8 sponge
9 tissues
10 mirror

G With what do most people shave?
In an old-fashioned razor there are…
After shaving you can use an…
When you shave with an old-fashioned razor you have to use a…
What do you use for cleaning your teeth?

G with an electric razor
razor-blades
after-shave lotion
shaving-brush and shaving-soap or shaving-cream
a tooth-brush and tooth-paste

H What things are there on the dressing-table for your nails? [4]
   And for your cheeks?
   And your lips?
   To smell nice?
   When you go on holiday you can put all these things in a...
   and take them with you.

H a nail-brush/a nail-file/nail-varnish/nail-scissors
   powder-puff
   lipstick
   perfume
   toilet bag

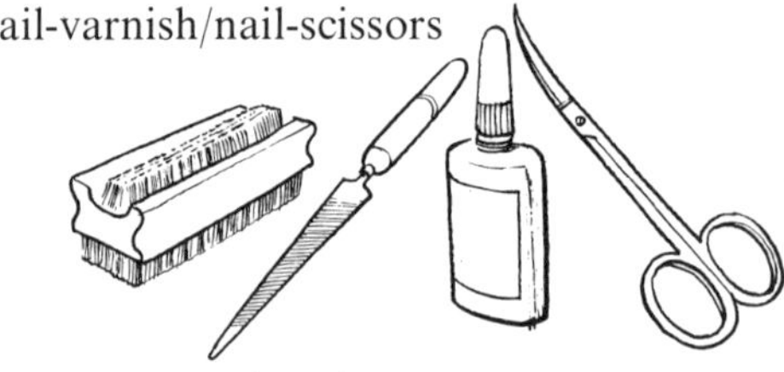

I 1 dressing-gown
   2 a pair of panties [pants]/briefs
   3 bra
   4 shirt
   5 socks
   6 stockings
   7 tights
   8 scarf

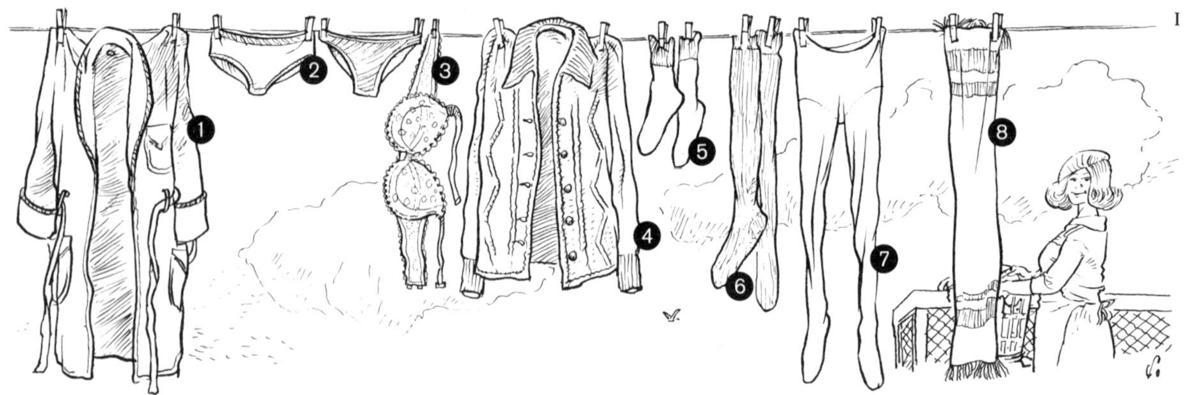

J *Give the opposite of:*
   a ready-made suit
   a short-sleeved dress
   this shirt can be ironed
   you can wash this coat

J
   a tailor-made suit
   a long-sleeved dress
   this is a non-iron shirt
   this coat needs dry cleaning

K With what do you brush your hair?
   You can also comb it with a...
   When you want a nice wave in your hair you can put in...
   When you are not satisfied with the colour of your hair you
   can...
   Bald people sometimes wear...

K with a hair-brush
   comb
   rollers

   dye it
   wigs or hair-pieces

L *Proverbs*
   Cut your coat according to your cloth.
   Borrowed clothes never fit well.

L Meaning

18 A talk about history

A
1 king
2 queen
3 castle
4 battlements
5 knight
6 page
7 herald
8 armour
9 lance
10 shield
11 sword

B This is a picture of a…

Tournaments were held in the…

A castle built in the Middle Ages is a…

Important periods in history are called…

Some of these periods are: [3]

We call a period of exactly one hundred years a…

When we haven't seen someone for a long time we can say:

B tournament

Middle Ages

mediaeval castle

Ages

the Stone Age – the Golden Age – the Elizabethan Age

century

I haven't seen you for ages.

C *Time chart*

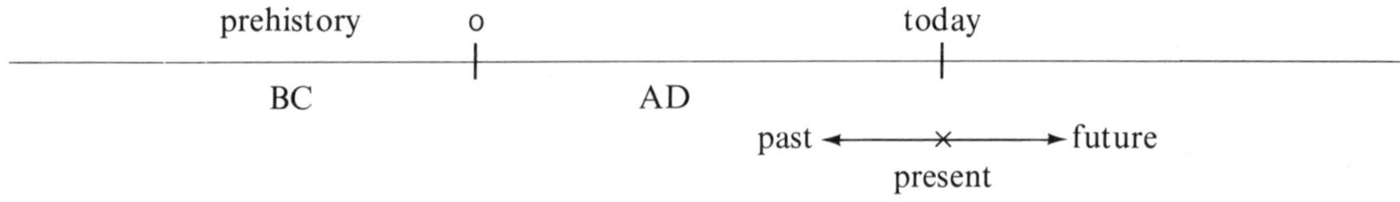

Things that have already happened took place in the...	past
Things that happen nowadays take place in the...	present
Things that are going to happen will take place in the...	future
We can divide time into shorter or longer periods.	
Name them. [8]	seconds/minutes/hours/days/weeks/months/years/centuries
The grammatical terms for 'time' in verbs is...	tense
What two auxiliary verbs are used to indicate future tense?	shall – will
So the future tense of 'to come is...	will [shall] come
The past participle of 'to tell' is...	told

D *History*

	D
The study of past events is called...	history
Somebody who has studied history is a...	historian
Something belonging to the past is called...	historical
Many people have ... furniture in their homes.	antique
Times very long ago are called...	ancient times [prehistory]
The study of everything connected with these ancient times is...	archaeology
We often put historical objects in a...	museum
Name some archaeological objects found in the ground: [3]	pottery/old jewellery/old arms [weapons]

E Many different peoples have lived in Britain in the course of history. Some of them are: [5]

	E They came from or lived originally in...
1 Britons	1 Brittany
2 Romans	2 Italy
3 Anglo-Saxons	3 Germany
4 Danes/Vikings	4 Denmark/Norway
5 Normans	5 Normandy [France]

F The Head of State in Britain is…
Kings, queens and emperors are all…
A country under the reign of a king or queen is a…
A country where they have a president is a…
The Queen and her family are called the…
The Queen's sons are…
Her daughter is a…
The eldest prince is the…
This means that he is the…
The Royal Family in Britain is from the House of…
The Romans had no king or president but an…
An emperor's territory is called an…

F the Queen
monarchs
monarchy
republic
Royal Family
princes
princess
Prince of Wales
heir to the throne
Windsor
emperor
empire

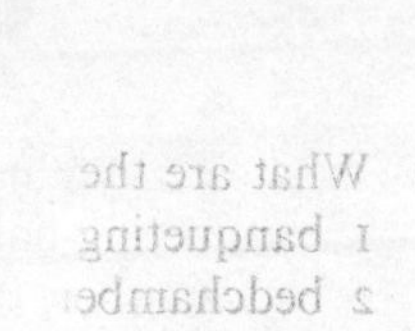

G 12 BC means…
1977 AD means…
AD stands for the Latin words…
In the Middle Ages there were campaigns to conquer the
Holy Land called…
People who tried to do so were…

G twelve years before Christ
1977 years after the birth of Jesus Christ
Anno Domini [the year of the Lord]

crusades
crusaders

H This castle looks…
Another name for this kind of castle is…
It's surrounded by a…
Across the moat there is a…
We can also see…
The small towers are called…
Nowadays most castles are in…

H magnificent
fortress
moat
drawbridge
towers and flags
turrets
ruins

I What are they used for?
1 banqueting-hall
2 bedchamber
3 dungeon

In a dungeon it's…
Sometimes the walls and floors are…
Being in such a dungeon is very…

J In the picture we see two…
They are statues of…
Statues are built as a…
The statue of **Lord Nelson** is in…
Gardens laid out in memory
of famous people are called…

I
1 to eat in
2 to sleep in
3 to keep prisoners in

dark and gloomy
damp [wet]
unhealthy

J statues
Lord Nelson and Queen Victoria
memorial of famous people
Trafalgar Square

memorial gardens

K Knights are…
People holding a special title [rank] belong to the…
Another word for nobleman is…
People without titles are called…

Here are the titles of some peers and their wives.
1 Duke
2 Marquis
3 Earl [British title]
4 Count [Foreign title]   generally called: 'Lord'
5 Viscount
6 Baron
7 Knight
8 Baronet   generally called: 'Sir'
9 Squire
The wife of a nobleman is called…

K noblemen
nobility/peerage
peer
commoners

1 Duchess
2 Marchioness
3 Countess
4 Countess
5 Viscountess
6 Baroness

Lady [+family name]

19 A birthday party

A
1 birthday cake
2 candles
3 streamers
4 decorations
5 presents
6 sausage rolls
7 sandwiches
8 sweets
9 jellies
10 drinks

This is a special day. It's someone's… birthday
Then you celebrate the day when… you were born
Mother has prepared all kinds of delicious foods and then… set the table [laid]

Say in a different way:
She has taken a lot of trouble she has put a lot of effort into the work
Mother does not want the house to be turned upside down mother does not want the house to be in a mess

B A way of asking people to your party is to send… B invitations [to invite]
For official occasions you say… I request the pleasure of your company
Invitation cards are delivered through… the letter-box
You should always reply to an invitation. That is… polite
Not to reply is… rude
If you are able to attend you reply with… an acceptance

If you can't come you reply with… a refusal
Another verb meaning 'to refuse' is… to decline [the offer]
When people just come in for a minute you can say… they dropped in
Some people dropped in unexpectedly means… some people came without being invited
At parties the guests often drink to someone's health. They propose… a toast
Cheers!
Some birthday songs are: Happy birthday to you
For he's a jolly good fellow

Here are some party games for younger children: musical chairs
pass the parcel
blindman's buff
When somebody does something silly we say… he is making a fool of himself
When a joke is very funny people… burst out laughing
The room is crowded means that it is… full of people
Guests are told to make themselves… comfortable

C **What are they doing?** C They are shaking hands
Mother *Friend*
May I introduce my son to you? It's his birthday. Oh, congratulations and many happy returns of the day. How old are you?

Boy *Friend*
I'm eighteen, still a teenager. My mother is 36. She is twice as old as I am. He has grown quickly.
He takes after his father.
I'm sorry, but I must go.
Remember me to your husband.
Give him my regards.

Mother
Drop me a line some time to keep in touch. Bye.

D *Name the opposite of:* D
to accept to decline [refuse]
polite impolite [rude]
to be born to die

E On your birthday you feel quite…
  You receive…
  What are surprise presents?
  When you give a birthday present you use special paper to…
  You like all your presents very much but the one you like
  best is your…
  You were given a motorcar and felt completely…
  Everyone at a party usually feels…
  The opposite of happy is…
  To beam with joy means…

E excited
  presents
  unexpected presents
  wrap it up

  favourite present
  overwhelmed
  cheerful/happy
  sad/unhappy
  to look very happy

F Before going to a party mother usually gives her child a few
  instructions. Here are some of them:

  When a party is over you say to the hostess…
  Mother asks: 'Did you enjoy yourself?'
  After the party the children have to go…
  Some are … by their parents.
  Some live very near, within…
  Sometimes the hostess takes some children in her car and…
  'Now that the party is over we had better turn in', means…

F
  behave yourself
  remember your manners
  say: please and thank you
  thank you for having me
  'Yes, thank you, I had a lovely time.'
  home
  fetched/collected
  walking distance
  drops them off at their homes
  we had better go to bed

G When an acquaintance dies and is buried we attend…
  At the head of the funeral procession we see…
  We offer our… to the relatives.
  The people attending the ceremony are called…
  The relatives of the deceased are in…
  Some other words connected with a funeral:

G his funeral
  the hearse
  condolences
  the mourners
  mourning

1 grave
2 tomb
3 gravestone/tombstone
4 coffin
5 wreath
6 cemetery/graveyard/churchyard

H Sometimes the body is not buried but…	H cremated [to cremate]
This is done in…	a crematorium
The atmosphere is…	solemn
The process of preserving the body from decay with oils and spices is known as…	embalming
The close relatives of the deceased are in a state of deep…	sorrow/grief
For them it's often difficult to … their emotions.	control
We say: this death has … them deeply.	affected [to affect]
A woman whose husband has died and who has not married again is…	a widow
A man whose wife has died is a…	widower
Children who have lost both their parents are…	orphans
Put differently: They felt sorry for her.	they pitied her [took pity on her].

20 A picnic in the woods

A In this picture the boys and girls are having a…
At home they have packed their food into a…
Now the meal has already been…
The food looks desirable. It is very…
Everyone is hungry. They have an…
Their stomachs feel…

A picnic
picnic-basket
laid out
appetizing
appetite
empty

B What have they brought with them?

B 1 a flask of tea/coffee
2 pieces of cheese
3 sausages
4 a jar of jam
5 a jar of honey
6 cream cakes
7 jelly
8 trifle
9 ham sandwiches
10 egg sandwiches
11 jam tarts
12 ice-cream
13 bottles of lemonade

C *Name the principal forms of the underlined verbs:*
The table was <u>laid</u>.
Please, <u>spread</u> some butter on the bread.
He can't <u>keep</u> his mouth shut.
I've <u>known</u> him for a long time.

C

lay – laid – laid
spread – spread – spread
keep – kept – kept
know – knew – known

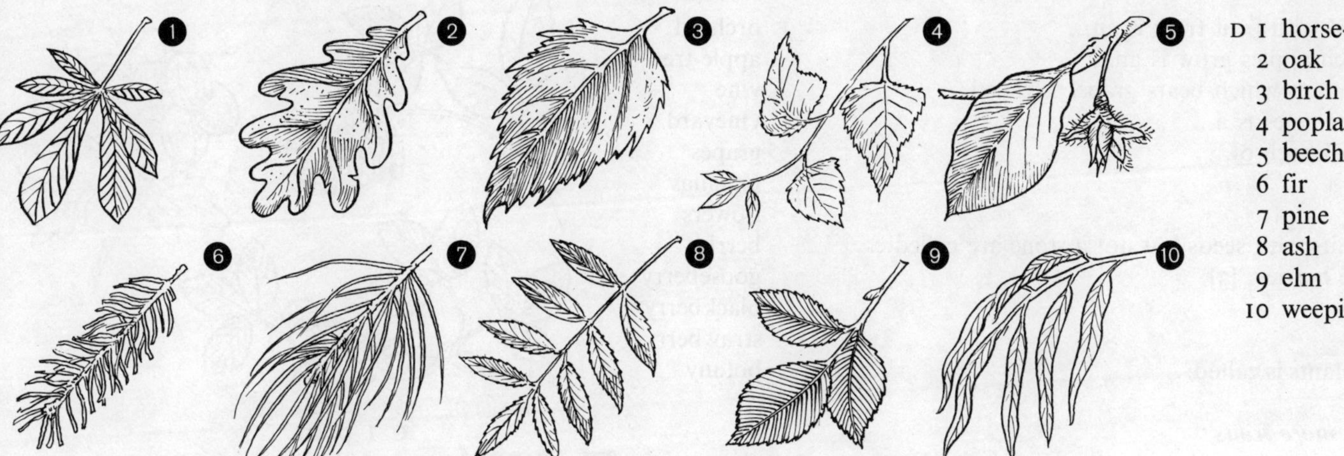

The nut or fruit of the oak is called an…	acorn
Another word frequently used for a horse-chestnut is a…	conker
Name some nuts: [5]	[sweet] chestnut/almond/hazelnut/peanut/coconut/beechnut

E	The scene of the picnic is set in…	E woodland
	So there are many kinds of…	trees
	The parts of a tree that grow down in the earth are the…	roots
	The main part of the tree is the…	trunk
	The outer part of the tree-trunk consists of…	bark
	A limb of the tree is a…	branch
	A small branch is a…	twig
	Very thick branches are called…	boughs
	In springtime… grow on the twigs.	buds
	They contain the unopened…	leaves or flowers
	In summer when the trees are full of flowers we say they are in…	blossom [bloom]
	The collective term for all the leaves is…	foliage
	Trees bearing cones, such as pine- and fir-trees, are called…	coniferous trees/conifers
	A tree which has green leaves all the year round is known as an…	evergreen
	Trees which shed their leaves annually are…	deciduous trees
	A woody plant is called a…	shrub/bush
	A small cluster of trees we call a…	copse/grove
	A large area of land covered with trees is a…	wood/forest

85

F A piece of land with fruit trees is an...
A tree on which apples grow is an...
The climbing-plant which bears grapes is called...
A plantation of vines is a...
We speak of a bunch of...

Some juicy fruits with seeds but not a stone are called...
Here are some berries: [3]

The study of plants is called...

F orchard
apple-tree
vine
vineyard
grapes
bananas
flowers
berries
gooseberry
blackberry
strawberry
botany

G *Here are some more fruits:*

   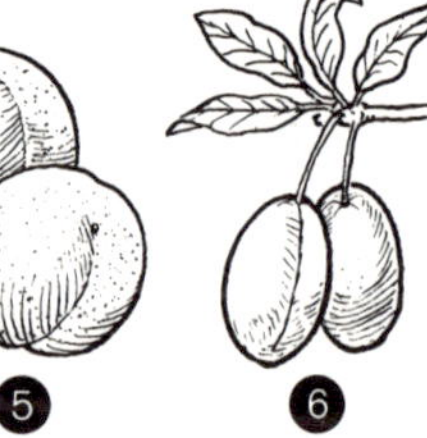 

G 1 pears
2 cherries
3 lemon
4 orange
5 peaches
6 plums
7 pineapple

Fruits may taste...

bitter, sour or sweet

H Which animals do we find around the wood?

H 1 deer [pl. deer]
2 squirrel
3 hare
4 frog
5 insect
6 bee
7 rabbit
8 mouse [pl. mice]
9 bird

21 A holiday at the seaside

A
1 fishing-boat
2 harbour
3 beach
4 seashore
5 lighthouse
6 cliffs
7 pier
8 beach-chair
9 bathing-costume
10 bikini
11 swimming-trunks
12 sunshade
13 wind-break
14 surf-board
15 surfer

B When we have a day or a few days off we call it a…
In summer we have…
At Christmas schoolchildren have…
Public holidays in England are called…
A place on the coast where you can spend your holidays is a…
Mention some Bank Holidays:

B holiday
summer holidays
Christmas holidays
Bank Holidays
seaside resort
Easter Monday/Whit Monday/Boxing Day/Last Monday in August

C What can you do at the seaside? [4]
When you lie in the sun for some time you get a…
Don't stay in the sun too long or else you may get…
The illness caused by too much sun is…

C lie in the sun, bathe in the sea, walk along the beach, go sailing
suntan
sunburnt
sunstroke

When the heat is too great you should sit in the...   shade
When the sun shines you can see the outline of your body
on the ground. That's your...   shadow

D Name some sports you can practise in or on the water. [7]   D swimming/sailing/waterskiing/diving/rowing/fishing/surfing

E People who go on holiday are...   E tourists/holiday-makers
Sometimes they stay at a...   hotel
Young people who don't want to spend too much money can
stay at a...   youth-hostel
When tourists stay at a hotel and have all their meals there
we say that they have...   full board
Otherwise it's...   bed and breakfast
When they have brought a tent or caravan they go...   camping
Then they stay at a...   camp-site
The road along the coast where people can walk is the...   promenade
There you can buy flowers, postcards and newspapers at...   kiosks or stalls
When it's hot you feel like...   a drink/refreshment
Some soft drinks are: [4]   pop/coke/orange juice/
                                                              lemonade
Name some spirits: [4]   cognac/gin/whisky/
                                                              brandy

F *Give the opposite of:*   F
a holiday   a working-day
salt water   fresh water
soft drinks   alcoholic drinks [spirits]
a sunny day   a dull day or rainy day

G *Weather conditions*

Britain has a wet…	climate
But in summer it's often…	warm/sunny
When it rains for a long time everything gets…	wet through
A light rain is called…	drizzle
When it's raining heavily we say…	it's pouring
When the rain or snow falls only for a short period of time we call it a…	shower
When the sun is not shining we say that it's…	cloudy/dull/overcast
After a very hot day there may be a…	thunderstorm
What we see then is…	lightning
And we hear…	thunder
Another word for a storm is a…	gale
A very violent wind is called a…	hurricane
A thick mist we call…	fog
Information about tomorrow's weather is called the…	weather-forecast
When the temperature is below zero we say that…	it's freezing
It's 30° C means…	it's thirty degrees centigrade
We can read the temperature on the…	thermometer
The barometer tells us…	what kind of weather we may expect

H *Give the principal forms of:*

to drink	drink – drank – drunk
to lie	lie – lay – lain
to shine	shine – shone – shone
to do	do – did – done
to freeze	freeze – froze – frozen

I *Children's rhyme*

When the windows are white with frost children say: Look out, look out, Jack Frost is about.

Proverbs

It never rains but it pours.
It's raining cats and dogs.

A *Introductions*

When you meet someone for the first time it is polite to...	shake hands
Then you say...	How do you do?
If it's someone you have met previously you may say...	How are you?
To which they will probably reply...	Very well, thank you.
Or less formal...	Fine thanks, and you?
When a boy meets his friends he says...	Hello/Hi!
At a social gathering [meeting] it's polite to...	introduce people
Another word for introducing people is...	presenting them [e.g. to the Queen]
Someone you don't know very well is an...	acquaintance of yours
After having met somebody for the first time you can say: I'm happy...	to have made your acquaintance
When you meet a person you know in the street it's polite to ... him.	greet

B *Dating*

Boy.
Would you like a cigarette?
Can I get you a drink?
Are you waiting for someone or are you free this evening?

Would you like to come out with me tonight?

I'll pick you up at your home at about 8.
Later that same evening.
May I take you home and can I see you again tomorrow?

Girl.
Thank you, have you got a light?
No, thanks.
I had an appointment to meet a friend here but he has not turned up.
I'd love to. Thank you. Where shall we meet and at what time?

Thank you, it's been a wonderful evening. I've enjoyed myself tremendously.

C *Opposites*

polite
kind
grateful/thankful
What a lovely day!
Isn't it cold today?
It's foggy, isn't it?

impolite/rude
unkind
ungrateful
What awful weather!
Isn't it hot today?
It's a clear day, isn't it?

D *Name the three principal forms of the underlined verbs:*
Don't <u>forget</u> old friends.
They <u>got</u> acquainted last year.
You usually <u>give</u> your hostess some flowers.
Let's <u>have</u> a drink.

forget – forgot – forgotten
get – got – got
give – gave – given
have – had – had

91

E People often gather in a club. There they meet the usual…   E circle of friends
When they join in the activities [i.c. games] everyone
chooses a…   partner
To be in the limelight means…   to receive great
                                                                      publicity
I'm sorry but I can't come because I've made another…   arrangement
Another word for arrangement used in this sense is…   appointment/date

F *Make your choice:*   F
On leaving someone it's correct to say: 'I'm delighted to have
met you/glad to know you'.   'I'm delighted to have met you.'
To be accompanied means to be alone/to be with another
person.   to be with another person
The person you are with is your company/companion.   companion
When somebody resembles his father in character or features
we say: 'He remembers his father/he takes after his father.'   'He takes after his father.'
Remember me to your mother means: convey my greetings to
your mother/help me to think of your mother.   convey my greetings to your mother
Keep in touch means: don't let me go/don't lose contact.   don't lose contact

G *Interviewing a tourist in London.*   G
Where do you come from?   I'm from Holland.
What part of Holland do you come from?   I'm from the west. From Amsterdam.
How long have you been here?   I've been here for a week now. I'm on holiday.
Is this your first visit?   No, I was here last year.
Are you enjoying your stay?   Yes, I like it very much.
Thank you for the interview.   Don't mention it.

H
pardon – repeat
hear
kind
care
interrupting – apologize
Do you mind
ahead
trouble

indeed

23 An accident

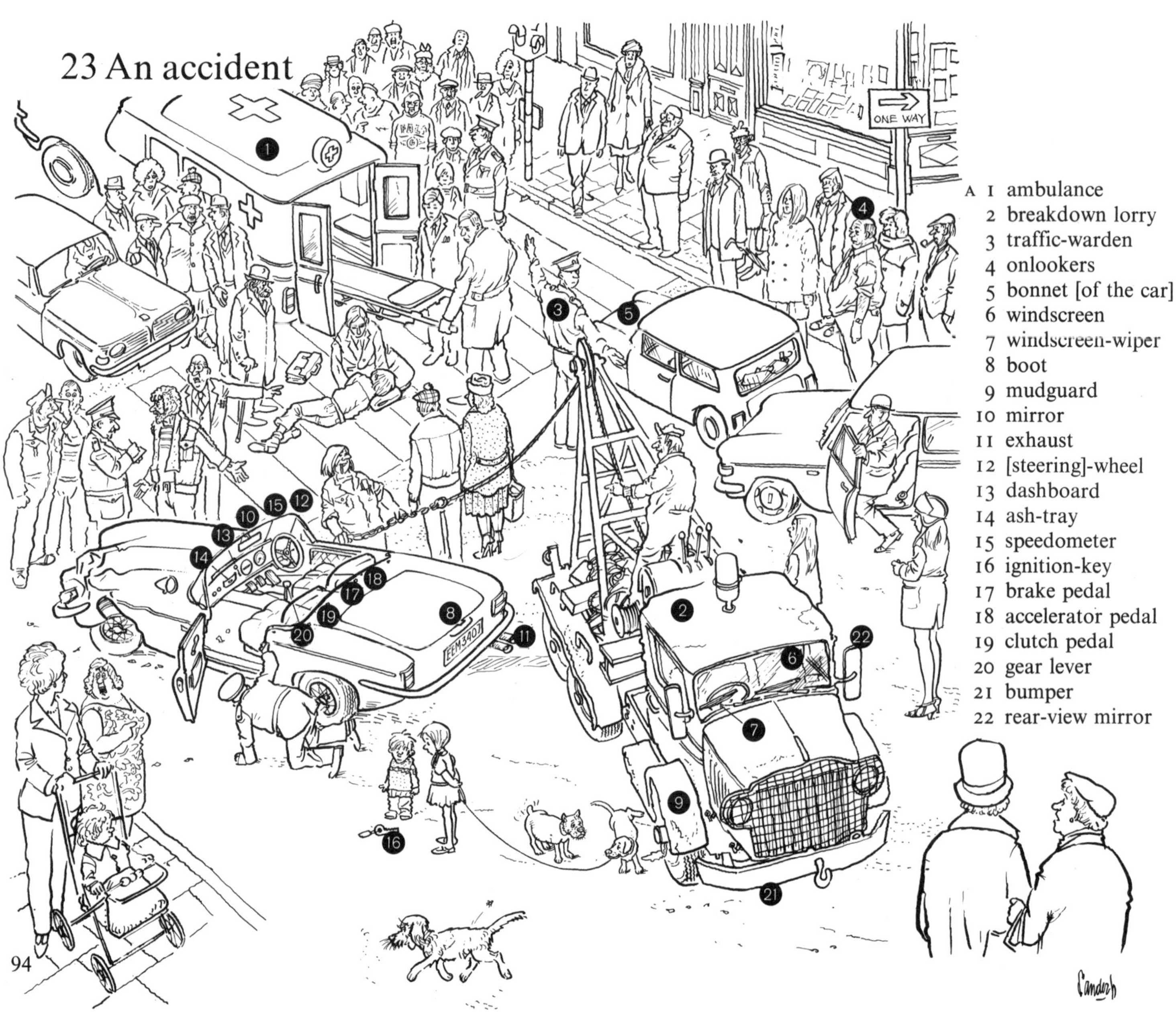

A 1 ambulance
2 breakdown lorry
3 traffic-warden
4 onlookers
5 bonnet [of the car]
6 windscreen
7 windscreen-wiper
8 boot
9 mudguard
10 mirror
11 exhaust
12 [steering]-wheel
13 dashboard
14 ash-tray
15 speedometer
16 ignition-key
17 brake pedal
18 accelerator pedal
19 clutch pedal
20 gear lever
21 bumper
22 rear-view mirror

B *Look at the picture*

In a busy shopping-street there has been an…	accident
The little boy [Gerald] has been…	knocked down
He is…	injured
He is lying…	unconscious
People who have seen it happen are…	witnesses
Others who just gather to see what has happened are…	onlookers
Some onlookers are hysterical. They begin to…	cry
Everyone is…	shocked
Who is helping Gerald?	an ambulance man
Gerald is taken to…	hospital
What's the traffic-warden doing?	he is directing the traffic
He tries to prevent a…	traffic-jam
When Gerald has been taken to hospital the crowd slowly…	disperses

C

What is the doctor doing?	He is examining Gerald.
When you are badly injured you need an…	operation
Who operates on people?	a surgeon
Gerald is only suffering from…	shock
His parents can see him during…	visiting hours
His friends will send him…	Get Well cards
Perhaps they will also send him…	flowers
Many flowers together we call a…	bunch [bouquet]
Who is looking after Gerald now?	the nurses
When Gerald is well again [has recovered] he will go…	home

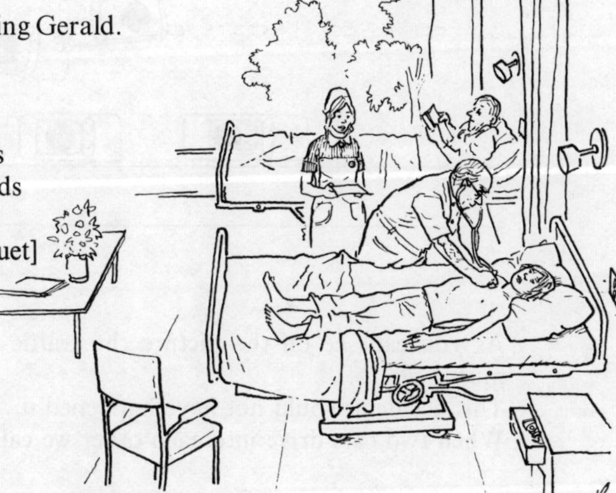

D *What nouns can be made from the following verbs?*

to operate	operation
to examine	examination
to happen	happening

E

Who was at fault?	the driver of the sportscar
Where did he knock the boy down?	on a zebra-crossing

The policeman asks for the driver's [3]

registration number [licence number]
driving licence
insurance certificate

The sportscar is...   damaged
It is taken to a...   garage
This is done by a...   breakdown lorry

F *Diagram of a common accident*

F

1 van pulling out
2 car swerving to avoid van
3 car overtaking others
4–5–6 parked cars
7–8–9 oncoming traffic

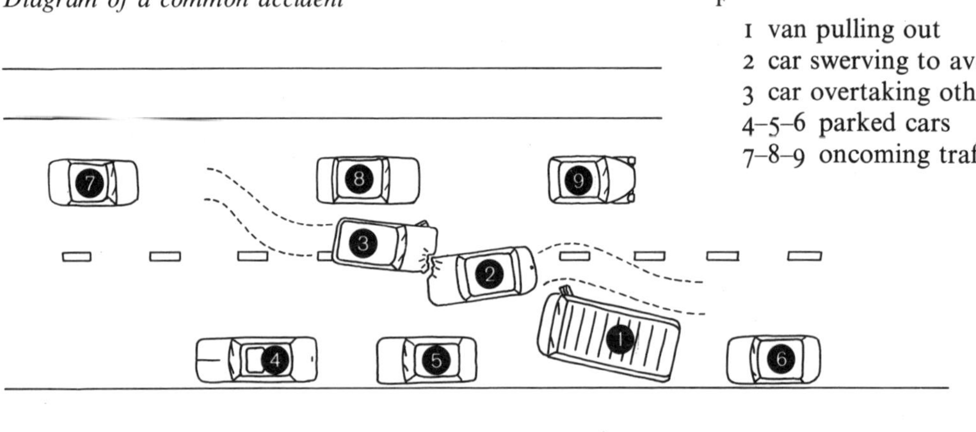

As you can see on the picture the traffic in Great Britain
must keep to...   the left
This accident would not have happened if...   the driver of the van had checked before pulling out
When two cars drive into each other we call that a...   collision

G *Give one word for:*
using the brakes
using the accelerator pedal
driving backwards

G

braking
accelerating
reversing

24 In the artist's studio

<table>
<tr><td>B In English the word artist mainly applies to…</td><td>B painters and sculptors</td></tr>
<tr><td>Drawing, painting and sculpting are together called…</td><td>the fine arts</td></tr>
<tr><td>A good picture or painting is a…</td><td>work of art</td></tr>
<tr><td>It has an … value.</td><td>artistic</td></tr>
<tr><td>The man or woman who made it is the…</td><td>artist</td></tr>
<tr><td>To become a good artist you have to be…</td><td>talented/gifted</td></tr>
<tr><td>The man who judges the artistic value of a work of art is an…</td><td>art-critic</td></tr>
<tr><td>Silk produced in factories is called…</td><td>artificial silk</td></tr>
<tr><td>It means that it is not real silk but…</td><td>imitation [to imitate]</td></tr>
<tr><td>The man who teaches art at school is the…</td><td>art-master</td></tr>
</table>

C This is a…

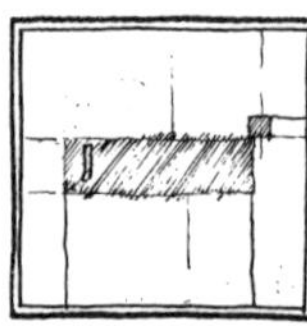

C palette

On the palette we see…
Of course the paint has different…
Name the colours of the rainbow:
Some other colours are: [5]
A picture with many colours is a…
What's a picturesque scene?

paint
colours
red/orange/yellow/green/blue/indigo/violet
brown/pink/purple/white/black
colourful picture
a scene that looks like a picture

D *Here are some arts. Name the artist.*
painting…
sculpture…
photography…
filming…

D

painter
sculptor
photographer
camera-man

E The shape of the first painting is…
But the second one is…
Some other shapes are: [3]

E square
rectangular
circular, triangular, oval

 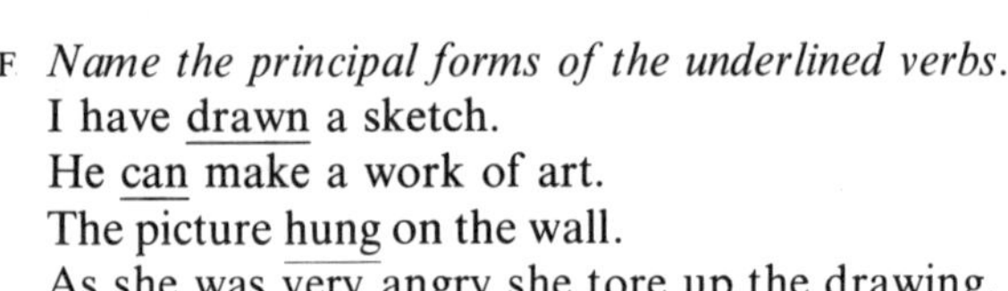   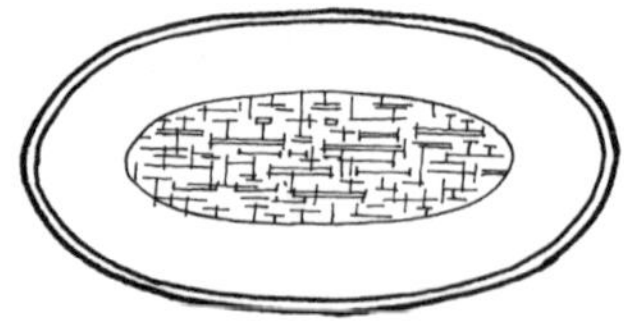

F *Name the principal forms of the underlined verbs.*
I have <u>drawn</u> a sketch.
He <u>can</u> make a work of art.
The picture <u>hung</u> on the wall.
As she was <u>very</u> angry she <u>tore</u> up the drawing.

F

draw – drew – drawn
can – could
hang – hung – hung
tear – tore – torn

G *At an art-gallery*

The man on the right is the…	owner of the gallery
He is an expert on…	art
The other people are…	visitors/clients
They have come to view the…	exhibition [to exhibit]
What kinds of pictures are shown here?	a landscape/a portrait/a still life
According to different techniques we can distinguish: [4]	etches/sketches/oil-paintings/engravings
Styles of painting often end in…	-ism
The best-known are…	impressionism and expressionism
When we look at a magnificent work of art we feel…	impressed by it

H *Photography*

First you must take the…	photo
Then the film must be…	developed
Then you can make a…	print [to print]
To make a photo bigger we must…	enlarge it
What else can be printed?	newspapers/magazines/books

I People who write poetry are…   I poets
Compositions in verse are called…   poems
The other writers write…   prose
Someone who writes novels is a…   novelist
Plays are written by a…   playwright
When a book is finished the author hopes it will be…   published
The firm which publishes the book is…   the publisher
The man who is responsible for the contents of a newspaper is the…   editor
The paper which appears in the morning is the…   morning edition
A paper contains many…   articles
Each page is divided into…   columns
A paper which comes out every day is a…   daily
The paper tells us about the…   events of the day
What do we call a paper which is published once a week?   a weekly
A magazine which appears every month is a…   monthly
On the first page of the paper we can see the…   main headlines

J *Put it differently:*   J
That's why poor people can't buy expensive paintings.   consequently poor people
We like excellent work.   we appreciate excellent work
Eternal fame.   immortal fame
Works of art are by no means cheap.   works of art are certainly not cheap

25 Do you like sailing?

A
1 crane
2 warehouse
3 dock
4 steamer
5 sailing-ship
6 bow
7 stern
8 portholes
9 funnel
10 railing
11 mast
12 mainsail
13 figure-head
14 rudder
15 tiller

B In the picture we see the...

Ships are loaded and repaired in...

They are loaded and unloaded by...

Ships which carry cargoes are...

Products like corn, sugar etc. are shipped in large quantities.

This kind of transport is called...

A ship used for war purposes is a...

A ship which carries passengers is a...

B dock area [dockyard]

docks

cranes

cargo-boats/freighters/container ships

bulk-transport

warship/man-of-war

passenger-ship

A ship which is part of a commercial fleet is called a…   liner
When passengers go on to a ship we say that they…   board the ship [embark]
One word for ships and boats is…   vessels
After a ship has sailed into the harbour it is…   moored [to moor]
This is mostly done with a…   rope/cable

C *Welcome on board*

When a ship goes out to sea it leaves the…   port/harbour
The speed of a ship is measured in…   knots
A holiday-trip by ship is a…   cruise
Behind the ship we see the…   coast
The coast in the picture consists of…   cliffs
They are…   steep rocks
There is a lighthouse on the cliffs used for…   warning ships at sea
When a ship hits the rocks it becomes a…   wreck
We say then: The ship is…   shipwrecked
Then the people on the ship may send an…   S.O.S. [save our souls]
On the coast a life-boat is launched to…   save the lives of the people on board
When your ship is wrecked you have to jump overboard. Then you should wear a…   life-jacket
When it's stormy weather the surface of the water begins to…   move
These movements of the water are called…   waves
When it's very hot weather we sometimes speak of a…   heat-wave
When the waves are very high many people get…   seasick
They suffer from…   seasickness
Then they hang over the rails and…   vomit/are sick

D *Name the opposite of:*
calm weather — stormy weather
the tide is in — the tide is out
it's high tide — it's low tide
starboard [right side of the ship] — port
above sea-level — below sea-level

E The man in command on board is the... — captain
The first mate is responsible for the... — navigation [to navigate]
Sea-maps are called... — charts
A captain knows where they are at sea by finding the... — longitude and latitude
To navigate a ship the sailors need a... — compass and other instruments
The man who is in charge of life-boats, anchor etc. is the.. — boatswain
Who serves the food? — the steward does
Who prepares the food on board? — the cook does
The food is prepared in the... — galley
The engineer looks after the... — engines
All the people who work on board are... — seamen [sailors]
Together they are called the... — crew of the ship
The sailors sleep in... — bunks/berths

F Each floor of a ship is called a... — deck [upper-deck/lower-deck]
Holidaymakers on board can sit in... — deck-chairs
They sleep in... — cabins
The foremost part of the ship is the... — bow
The name of a ship is often painted on the back. This part of a ship is called the... — stern
The rudder is used to... — steer the ship
The goods are stored in the... — hold
When you want to leave the ship you have to use the... — gang-plank [gang-way]

G *Fishing-gear*
For fishing you need: [5] — a fishing-rod/a line/a hook/a float [to float]/some bait
When you are angling you try to... — catch a fish
When you fish in a river you may catch... — freshwater-fish
Then you need a... — fishing-licence/permit
When you fish in the sea you can only catch... — saltwater-fish [sea-fish]

Here are some freshwater-fishes: [6]

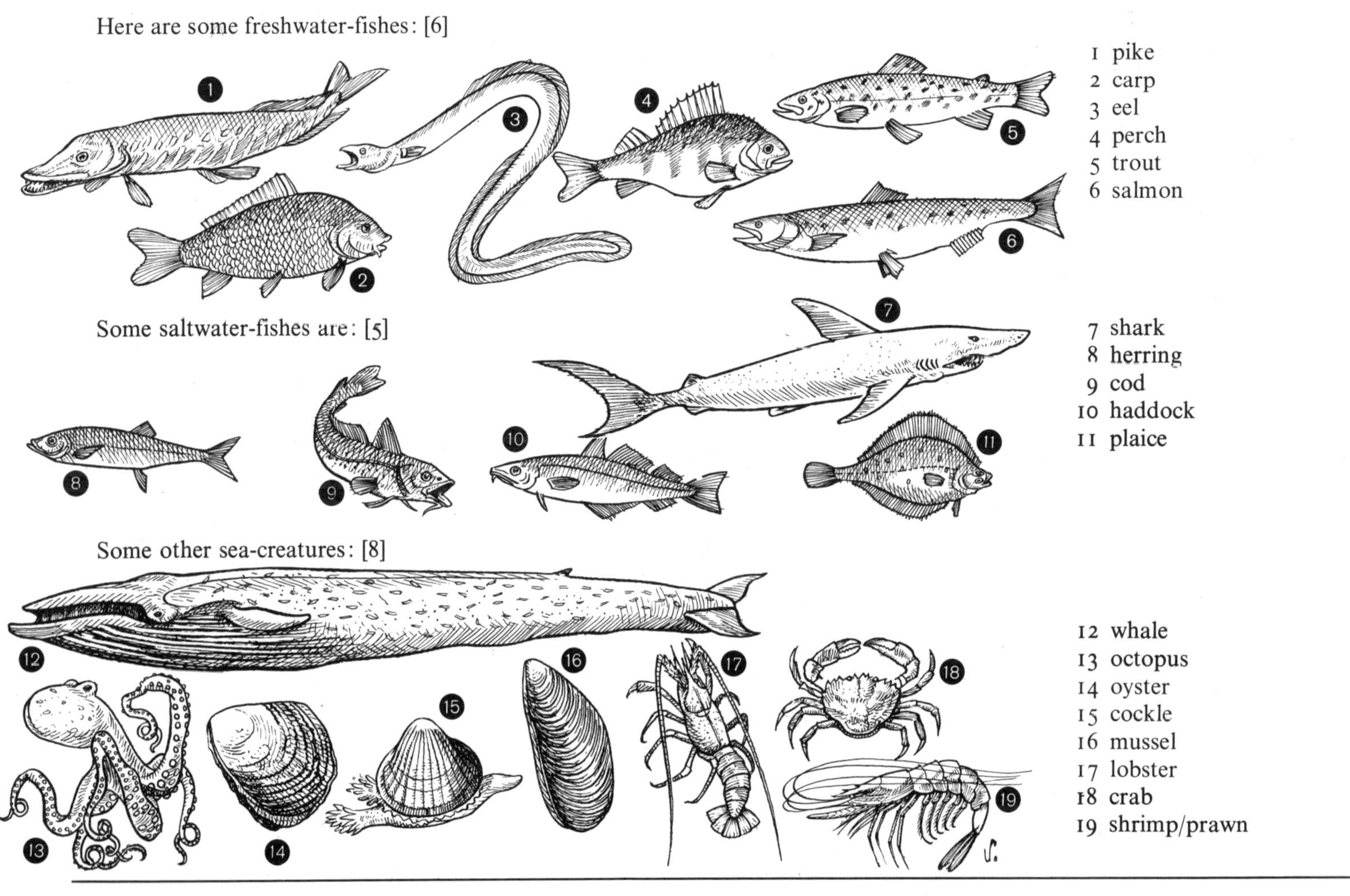

1 pike
2 carp
3 eel
4 perch
5 trout
6 salmon

Some saltwater-fishes are: [5]

7 shark
8 herring
9 cod
10 haddock
11 plaice

Some other sea-creatures: [8]

12 whale
13 octopus
14 oyster
15 cockle
16 mussel
17 lobster
18 crab
19 shrimp/prawn

H A man who catches fish for a living is a…
Most fishermen have…
When you fish for a hobby you can use a…
What do you row your boat with?

H fisherman
fishing-boats [trawlers]
rowing-boat
with oars

104

Some other types of boats are:

1 canoe
2 motorboat
3 dinghy
4 coaster
5 tanker
6 water-bus
7 ferry
8 tug
9 submarine
10 inflatable [dinghy]

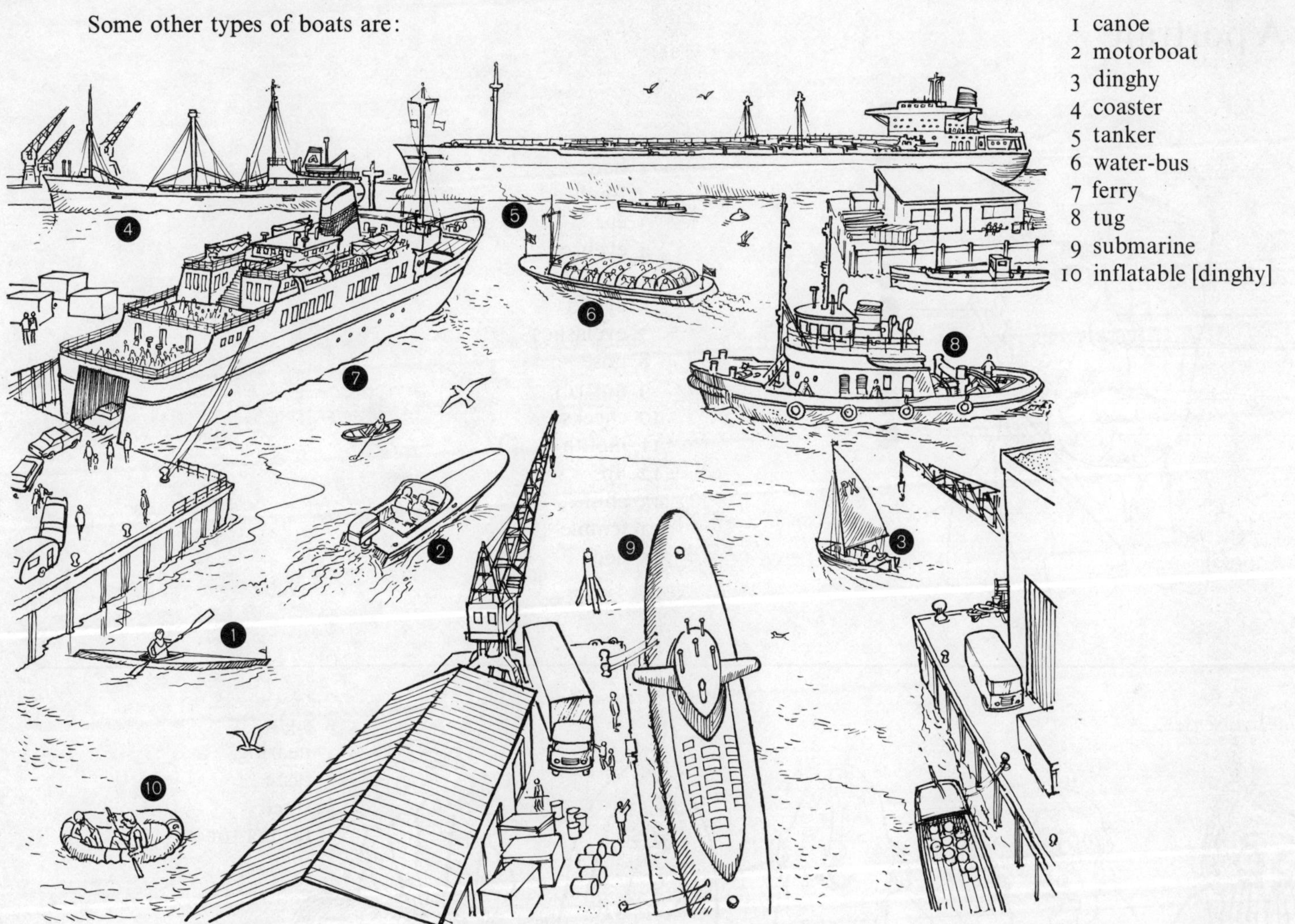

26 A portrait

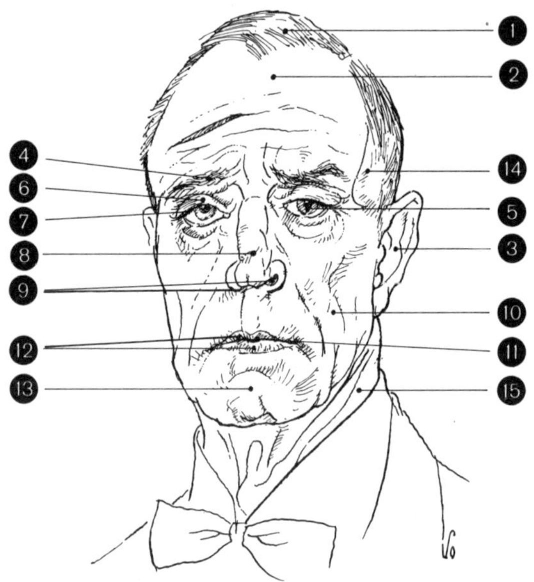

A
1 hair
2 forehead
3 ear
4 eyebrow
5 eye
6 eyelid
7 eyelashes
8 nose
9 nostrils
10 cheeks
11 mouth
12 lips
13 chin
14 temple
15 neck

B *The five senses:*

B sight
hearing
taste
smell
feeling/touch

C When you can't see you are…
   When you can only see through one eye…
   Going blind means…
   When you can't see well you have to wear…
   Short-sighted means that you can't…
   Long-sighted means that you can't…
   When you can't hear you are…

C blind
   you are partially blind
   gradually losing your sight
   glasses or contact lenses
   see well in the distance
   see objects which are too close to your eyes
   deaf

D *Make your choice:*
   To work well you must be healthy/ill.
   A rather fat woman is called a plump/thin woman.
   It's not healthy to be slim/stout.
   You chew with your jaws/teeth.
   On your feet there are toes/fingers.
   Your tongue/liver is in your mouth.
   When you breathe you use your lungs/kidneys.
   The outside of your body is called your skin/nerve.
   Another word for to sweat is to transpire/to perspire.
   A temperature is another word for health/fever.
   Arms and legs are called limbs/veins.
   When you are strong you have many muscles/brains.

D

   healthy
   a plump woman
   stout
   teeth
   toes
   tongue
   lungs
   skin
   to perspire
   fever
   limbs
   muscles

E 1 palm of the hand
   2 thumb
   3 index [forefinger]
   4 middle finger
   5 ring finger
   6 little finger
   7 nail
   8 knuckle
   9 wrist
   10 elbow

F *Give the principal forms of:*
to fall
to feel
to hear
to see

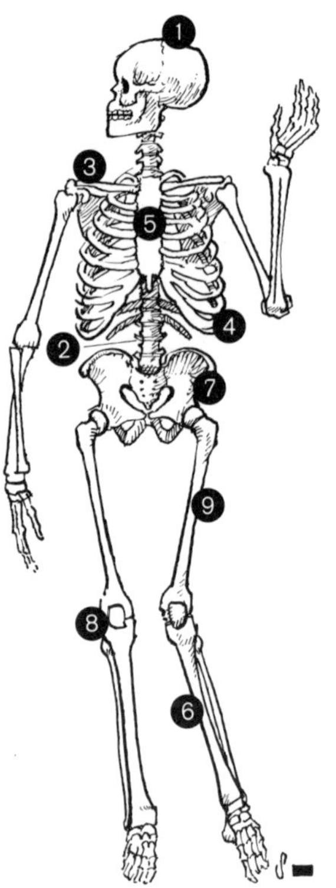

F
fall – fell – fallen
feel – felt – felt
hear – heard – heard
see – saw – seen

G 1 skull
2 spine/backbone [vertebral column]
3 collar-bone
4 ribs
5 breastbone
6 shin [-bone]
7 pelvis
8 knee-cap
9 thigh-bone

H The body consists of three important parts. Name them.

The place where two bones meet is a...
Inside the skull are the...
On the outside of a man's head grow[s]...

H head
trunk
limbs [arms and legs]
joint
brains
hair
beard
moustache

I When you have caught a cold and something tickles inside I sneeze
your nose you have to…
When something irritates your throat you have to… cough
When small children feel ill they often… cry/weep
When you are taken ill you… send for the doctor
He examines you and asks: how do you feel?
Your answer can be: I feel… [5] shivery/sick [squeamish]/faint/dizzy/depressed [down]

What sort of pain is it? [5] a dull pain/a sharp pain/a constant pain/a spasmodic pain/
pins and needles

When your throat hurts and it's difficult to swallow you
say:… I've a sore throat
When you have a pain in your head you say:… I've a headache

J The doctor feels your… J pulse
When he knows the symptoms he gives his… diagnosis
Then he may prescribe some… medicine
Some kinds of medicine are: [5] pills
capsules
powders
potions [mixtures]
ointment

When you have an infection the doctor will give you an… antibiotic
Then you will soon… recover
When you have recovered we say that the doctor has… cured his patient
A family doctor is also called a… general practitioner [GP]

K *Other parts of the body*

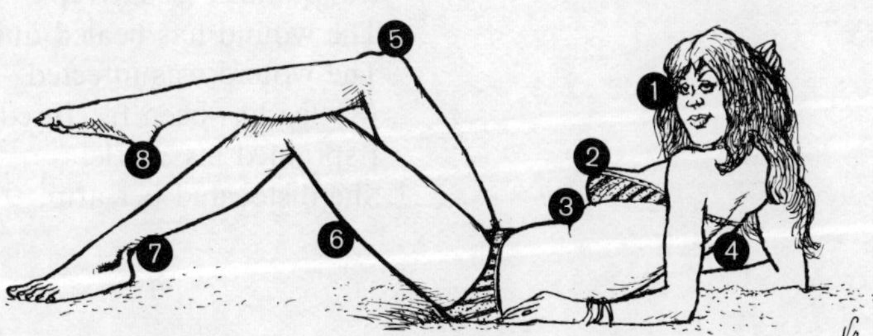

K 1 face
2 chest [breast]
3 stomach [belly]
4 back
5 knee
6 thigh
7 ankle
8 heel

L *Make adjectives from:*
nerve
pain
hygiene

Opposites:
man
male
masculine

M Here are some more illnesses/diseases. [6]

Children are vaccinated [get injections] against: [5]

N When you eat you put the food into your...
There you have to ... it.
Then it goes down your...
It enters your...
From the stomach it goes into the...
There the food is passed into the...
This system of using up the food is called...
The blood runs through your...
Food is the ... for your body.
It gives you...

O *Make sentences using the following words:*
nervous

to heal
to infect
to fracture [break]
to sprain
to dislocate

L
nervous
painful [painless]
hygienic

woman
female
feminine

M measles/scarlet fever/chicken-pox/mumps/pneumonia
[inflammation of the lungs]/flu [influenza]
smallpox/diphtheria/tetanus/measles/whooping-cough

N mouth
chew
throat
stomach
intestines
blood
digestion
veins and arteries
fuel
energy

O

When some people feel nervous they use a
tranquillizer [sedative].
The wound has healed quickly.
The wound was infected.
My leg has been fractured.
I sprained my ankle.
She dislocated her arm.

P When your leg is broken we speak of a…   P fracture
When your skin is slightly marked by something we
speak of a…   scratch
When you hurt yourself with a knife we speak of a…   cut/a wound
When you are bitten by an insect we say that you have had a…   bite
Sharp pain caused by a wasp is called a…   sting
If you stand too close to the fire you may get a…   burn

27 At the Post Office

A 1 counter
   2 safe
   3 telephone kiosk
   4 telephone
   5 receiver
   6 telephone directory
   7 stamp-machine

B *At the Post Office*
   What can you do at the Post Office? [4]

B Buy stamps
   Post letters or postcards
   Make a telephone call
   Send a telegram [wire] [Am. cable]

Another word for the post is the…   mail
Each letter or postcard must have a…   [postage] stamp
The money you have to pay for the stamp is the…   postage
The man who delivers the letters is the…   postman
On the pillar-box you find the time of…   collection
The man in charge of the post office is the…   postmaster

C *Sending a letter*
Where do you buy writing-paper?   at the stationer's
Putting your name at the end of a letter is called…   signing a letter
The name you put there is your…   signature
Before mailing it you must put the letter in an…   envelope
What do you write on the back of the envelope?   your own address [the address of the sender]
What do you write on the front of the envelope?   the name and address of the addressee
What do you stick on the letter then?   a stamp
Then you put the letter in a…   pillar-box
The place where the postman delivers your private mail is the…   letter-box
Big firms often have a P.O.B. That is a,..   post[office] box [a box-number]
You can send your letter [by] [3]   ordinary mail [first or second class]
   express [special delivery]
   as registered mail
Newspapers and magazines sent by post are called…   printed matter

D *Give the principal forms of:*
to send   send – sent – sent
to say   say – said – said
to put   put – put – put

E *Making a telephone call*
When you make a telephone-call you lift the…   receiver
Then you…   dial the number
If you don't know the number you can look it up in the…   [telephone] directory
When you can't find it there you can dial…   directory inquiries
Making a call to a place far away is called a…   long-distance call or a trunk call
To most countries in Europe you can phone…   direct
Then first dial the…   international code-number

If you have not got enough money you can ask for a person to person call and...   have the charges reversed

That means that the receiver of the call...   has to pay for it

When there is a difficulty with the connection the operator may tell you to...   hold the line

When the person we want to call is already speaking to someone else we say that...   the line [number] is engaged

When the phone is not working we say...   it's out of order

F *Give the opposite of:*
a trunk call   a local call
to send a picture postcard   to receive a picture postcard
to save money   to spend money

G Post Office Savings Bank means that...   you can deposit or withdraw money from an account there
Money can be sent by post in the form of a...   postal order [money order]
The money in a country is called the...   currency
How much one currency is worth in terms of another depends on the...   rate of exchange
If you have no cash on you, you can pay...   by cheque
People travelling abroad often use...   travellers' cheques
Cheques are kept in a...   cheque-book
When you pay by cheque you must also show your...   banker's card
Everyone who puts money in a bank must have or open an...   account
The money you have in a bank is your...   balance/credit
The sum of money which is owed to a bank is the...   debt
The bank sends you a list of transactions called a...   statement
When you have used up more money than there is on your account the statement will show an...   overdraft

H *What's the meaning of:*
She is blue   she is sad/depressed
He is yellow   he is a coward
They are in a brown study   they are deep in thought
He is in the red   he owes money to the bank [overdraft]

28 Shopping

A 1 counter
2 cash-desk
3 elevator/lift
4 escalator
5 customer[s]
6 assistant
7 shopping-bag
8 advertisement
9 manager
10 revolving door

B A large shop selling all kinds of goods is a...   B department store
When you enter some shops the doorbell...   rings
The goods are laid out on the...   counters
You can buy these goods. They are...   for sale
The goods they sell are called the...   merchandise
People standing in a row awaiting their turn are...   queueing up
When something costs a lot of money we say that it is...   expensive
The opposite of expensive is...   cheap
When an article is good and very cheap we say it's a...   bargain
When you have bought something you get a...   bill
You can pay at the...   cash-desk
The money that is the difference between the cost and the
money you offer in payment is your...   change

C What counters can you see in the picture? [5]   C a toy counter
   a watch and jewellery counter
   a counter full of things for the garden
   a counter with sweets and chocolates
   a counter full of household goods
Name some other departments: [4]   the clothes department
   the shoe department
   the book department
   the hosiery department

D The departments are on different...   D floors
The toy counter is on the...   ground floor
The book department is downstairs in the...   basement
The shoe department is...   upstairs
It is on the...   first floor
The clothes department is on the...   second floor
Another word for floor is...   storey

E *In what department would you expect to find the following*   E
things:
hats in the...   millinery department
stockings, tights and socks   hosiery department

F *Give the principal forms of the following irregular verbs:*
to ring
to wear
to cost
to pay

G *Conversation between shop-assistant and customer.*
Assistant
What can I do for you madam?
What size do you take?
Any special preferences?
Will these do?
Of course.

Customer
I'd like a pair of brown shoes, please.
Size five.
Yes, I like outdoor shoes, the latest type.
I think so. May I try them on?

These pinch my toes a little.

You want a larger size.
These shoes fit you.
Shall I wrap them up?
Is there anything else I can do for you?
You can pay at the cash-desk.
You're welcome, goodbye.

Yes, please.
No, thank you, that will be all.
Thank you for your assistance.

H Shops where you can help yourself are…
When there are many people in the shop you are sometimes…
The … is stamped on the things you buy.
On the label of the product you generally find the…
They weigh things on…
One thousand grams is a…
When an article is good we say that it is of…
The department where you can buy things to eat is the…
When an article is not there we say that it is not…

H self-service shops
pushed about
price
weight or the size
scales
kilogram
good quality
food department
in stock

Then the shopkeeper can...   order it for you
That doesn't cost any more. We say then...   it's all part of the service
When a shopkeeper earns money he makes a...   profit
A shopkeeper buys his goods from a...   wholesale dealer
Then the shopkeeper is the...   retailer

I   *Coins and banknotes*
£2 means...   two pounds
14 p means...   fourteen pence
£1 equals...   100 pence
1 shilling equals...   5 pence
What coins do you see on the picture?   1 penny
    5 pence
    10 pence
    50 pence
What banknotes do you see?   a one pound note
    a five pound note [a fiver]
    a ten pound note
That book costs one sixty-five means...   it costs one pound and sixty-five pence
When we have ten coins of one penny we say...   we have ten pennies
If we only think of the value we say...   we have ten pence
To change a pound means...   to give back coins to the value of one pound
If you don't possess much money you should be...   economical
Buying unnecessary things is...   wasting money
When you are careful with your money you are...   thrifty

J   *Expressions*
Money makes the man but manners make the gentleman.
Look after your pennies and the pounds will look after themselves.

29 'Join the army'?

B In Britain, when you are 17 you can…   B join the army
In Britain there is no…   conscription
So all soldiers are…   volunteers
Only in times of war do you get…   called-up [Am. draft]
What must a soldier do in a war?   defend his country

A great number of soldiers together we call an...   army
A fight between armies is a...   battle
The place where it all happens is the...   battlefield
Here are some weapons: [5]   pistol/revolver/rifle/cannon/[machine-]gun
Another word for weapons is...   arms
Most weapons are loaded with...   bullets
Bullets and shells together are called...   ammunition
In a war there are many...   casualties
This means that many people are...   killed or wounded
World War I is also called...   the Great War
A war between citizens of the same nation is a...   civil war
When armies stop fighting at the end of a war we
speak of an...   armistice [truce]
Afterwards the countries involved talk terms and make an
agreement called a...   treaty [of peace]
Freedom from war is...   peace
A violent overthrow of a system of government is a...   revolution [French Revolution]

C Our defence system consists of: [3]   C the army
    the navy
    the airforce

All people in the British army are...   soldiers
Every soldier has a certain...   rank
When you join the army you start as a...   private
After some time you can become a...   corporal
Non-commissioned officers are: sergeant

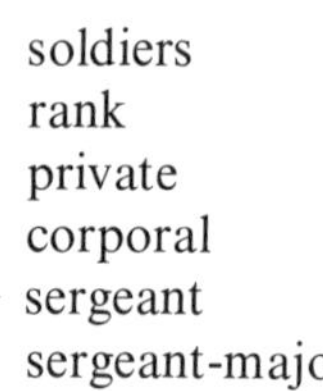

    sergeant-major

Some of the commissioned officers are: [5]
In World War II the rank of Montgomery was…
He was the highest in command. He was…
The most important officers form together the…
All soldiers have to … their superior officers.
Soldiers have to wear…

lieutenant/captain/major/colonel/general
field-marshal
commander-in-chief
staff
salute
caps and uniforms

D *Name the verb connected with the following nouns:*
a commander
an attack
a defence
a surrender
a declaration [of war]
a defeat
an invasion
a decision
captivity

D
to command
to attack
to defend
to surrender
to declare
to defeat
to invade
to decide
to capture

E An army is sub-divided into…
A large unit is a…
A small unit is a…
Name some other units: [4]
What's the parade-ground used for?

E units
regiment
platoon
squadron/company/battalion/section
for drilling and holding parades

F *Give the opposite of:*
war
friendly
cowardly
to lower a flag
backward[s]
a defeat
a friend

F
peace
hostile/unfriendly
courageous/brave
to hoist a flag
forward[s]
a victory
an enemy/a foe

G

   the allies

   a treacherous deed

   to discourage

   a siege

H The tanks are in full...
  One tank is...
  This is due to a mine which has...
  Fighting here requires much...
  All the time the soldiers are in great...
  In the air are bombers. They drop their...
  This is called an...
  Some soldiers are looking for...
  We can also say that they are looking for...

H action
  blown-up
  exploded
  courage
  danger
  bombs
  air-raid
  shelter
  protection

122

I *Name the principal forms of the underlined verbs.*
The bullet <u>hit</u> only his cap.   to hit – hit – hit
They <u>fought</u> with determination but they had to surrender.   to fight – fought – fought
The corporal was badly <u>hurt</u>.   to hurt – hurt – hurt
After their escape the P.O.W.'s [prisoners of war] <u>hid</u> in a
barn.   to hide – hid – hidden

J *Some words connected with 'war'.*
At the first shot the guard was…   alarmed
The night's rest of all the soldiers was…   disturbed
Someone who makes a person suffer is…   cruel
When there is no more hope you are…   desperate
This means that you are…   at a loss what to do
If an escaped P.O.W. was recaptured a terrible … would be his.   fate
It was a great … for the citizens that the war was over.   relief
Someone who has been very brave in the war is called a…   hero

K When someone runs away from his regiment in time of war
he is a…   deserter
When he is caught he has to appear before a military court of
law called a…   court-martial
People who refuse to fight on religious or other moral grounds
are…   conscientious objectors [conchies]
People who tell secrets to the enemy or work for the enemy
are called…   traitors/spies
The crime they commit is…   treason
People who try to get information from the enemy secretly
are known as…   spies [sing. spy]

L After a victory everybody flies the…   flag
The flags fly from…   flagpoles [mast-heads]
To pull up the flag is called…   to hoist the flag
When an important person has died the flags are flown at…   half mast
At sunset the flags are…   lowered

30 Home is home

A *You come to see a friend*
At the door you ring…
You wait on…
The door opens and your friend says:
On the doormat you…
Then you enter…
Your friend closes [shuts]…
A … leads to the first floor.
Your friend takes you into…
He opens the door and…

A
the bell
the doorstep
'Do come in!'
wipe your feet
the hall
the front-door
flight of stairs [staircase]
the living-room
shows you in

B *In the living-room*
1 table
2 chair
3 armchair
4 floor
5 ceiling
6 carpet
7 picture
8 settee
9 door
10 lampshade
11 standard lamp
12 cushion
13 vacuum cleaner
14 window

1 candle
2 candlestick
3 ash-tray
4 pipe
5 cigar
6 cage
7 parrot
8 jug
9 fireplace [open fire]

---

c What do you do first when you want to smoke a cigarette? c you take one out of the packet
Then you strike… a match
And you… light your cigarette
Instead of a match you can also use… a lighter
'It's unhealthy to inhale' means… it's unhealthy to breathe in the smoke

---

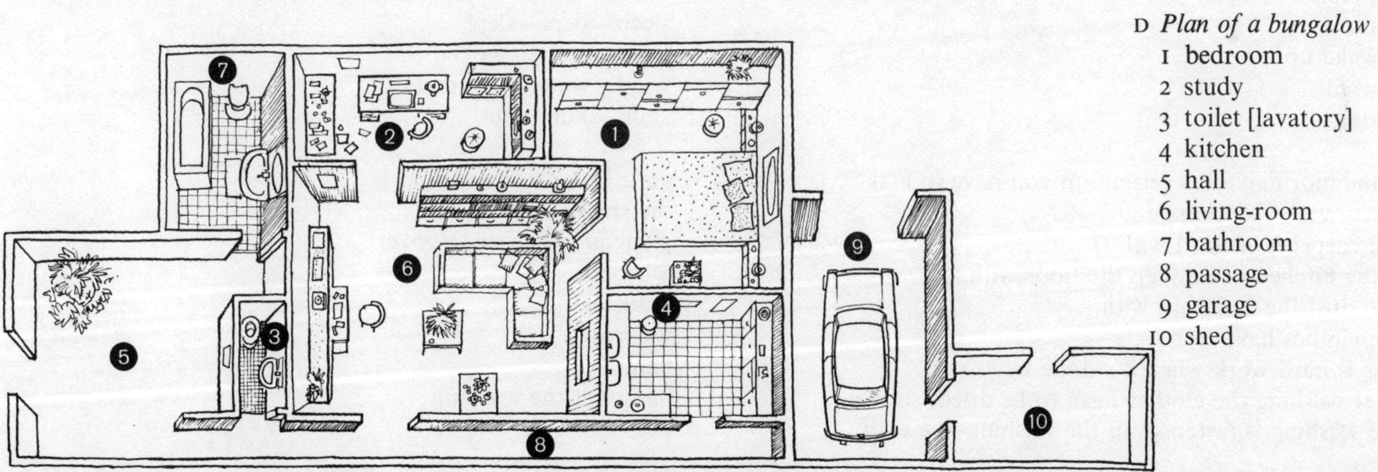

D *Plan of a bungalow*
1 bedroom
2 study
3 toilet [lavatory]
4 kitchen
5 hall
6 living-room
7 bathroom
8 passage
9 garage
10 shed

E Name some more rooms: [5]
What's a cellar used for?
What's a nursery?
What's a basement?

E sitting room [lounge in hotel] nursery/cellar/loft [attic]
to store food and drink [wine-cellar]
a room for children to sleep and play in
a floor below ground-level

F *Name the principal forms of:*
to sweep
to sleep
to wake up
to wind
to shut

F
sweep – swept – swept
sleep – slept – slept
wake – woke – woken
wind – wound – wound
shut – shut – shut

G In the morning after getting up you have to make...
Every week you change...
The carpet is cleaned with...
In the kitchen you sweep the floor with...
You dust the furniture with...
The clothes have to be...
This is hard work when it's done by...
After washing the clothes have to be dried, so you...
The washing is fastened on the washing-line with...

G your bed
the sheets
a vacuum cleaner [Hoover]
a broom
a duster
washed
hand
hang out the washing
pegs

Washing is much easier when you have...   an automatic washing-machine
When the clothes are dry they need...   ironing
Some clothes are torn and need...   mending
Most people do their sewing on...   a sewing-machine
Socks with holes in them have to be...   darned
After all this work has been done everything is... neat and clean

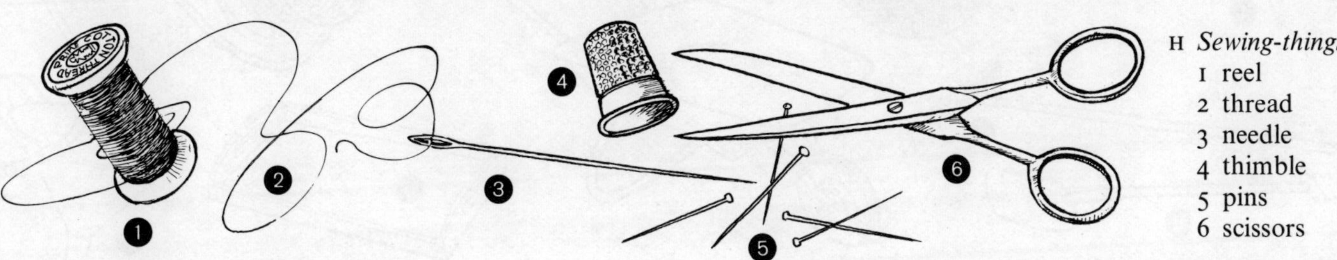

I *Give the opposite of:*

clean	dirty
above	below
over	under
in front of	behind
simple	complicated

J *Make your choice:*

around/beyond means 'further than' — beyond

to arrange flowers means to pick flowers/to put flowers into a vase — to put flowers into a vase

When you lock the door you use a key/a door-handle — a key

In a study you sometimes find a typewriter/refrigerator — a typewriter

K *In the bedroom*

A bed for one person is... — a single bed

A bed for two people is... — a double bed

What do we find on the bed? — a mattress/sheets/blankets [or a quilt]/pillows/a bedspread

You put the pillow in... — a pillow-case [pillow-slip]

Where do you keep your clothes? — in the wardrobe and in the chest of drawers

Combs, brushes and make-up are on...   the dressing-table
In the bedroom you can have a wash in...   the wash-basin
But when you want to take a bath or shower you go to...   the bathroom

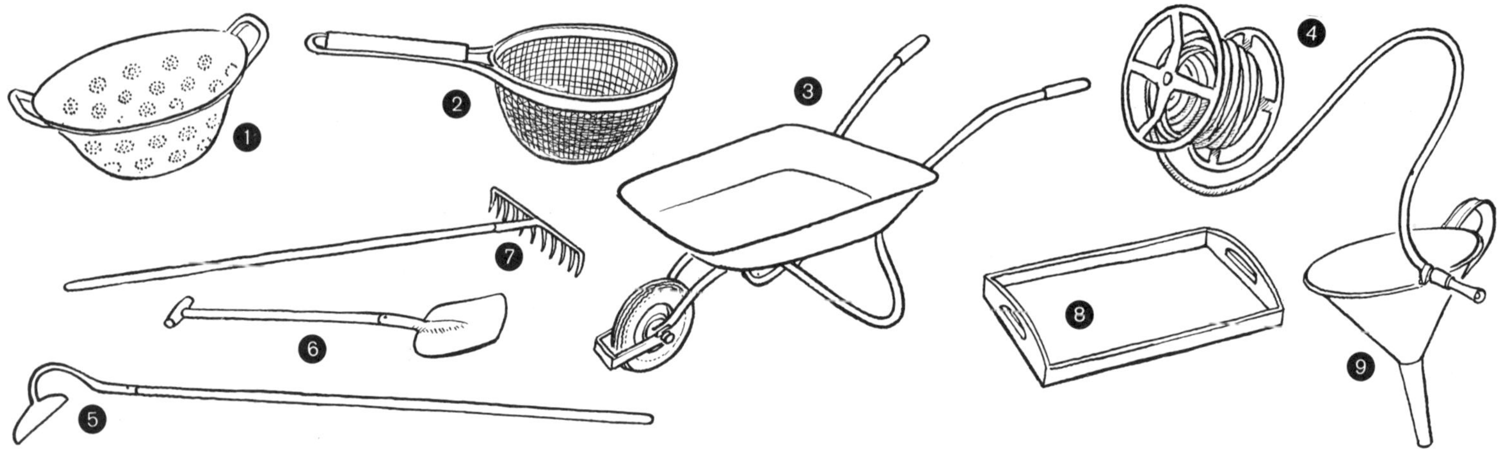

L *What are these for?*
   1 a colander   for straining vegetables
   2 a sieve   for sifting flour
   3 a wheelbarrow   for wheeling heavy loads
   4 a hose   for watering the flowers
   5 a hoe   for removing the weeds
   6 a spade   for digging the garden
   7 a rake   for gathering garden rubbish
   8 a tray   for carrying things on
   9 a funnel   for putting liquids in bottles

M What kinds of heating can you use in a house? [4]   M central heating/open fire/oil heater/gas or electric fires
   Can you name some kinds of fuel? [5]   wood/oil/coal/gas/electricity
   When it's dark outside you have to turn on...   the lights
   If you want to put on the lights you...   switch them on
   But table-lamps have to be...   plugged in
   In shopwindows, schools etc. we often find...   fluorescent lamps [strip lighting]

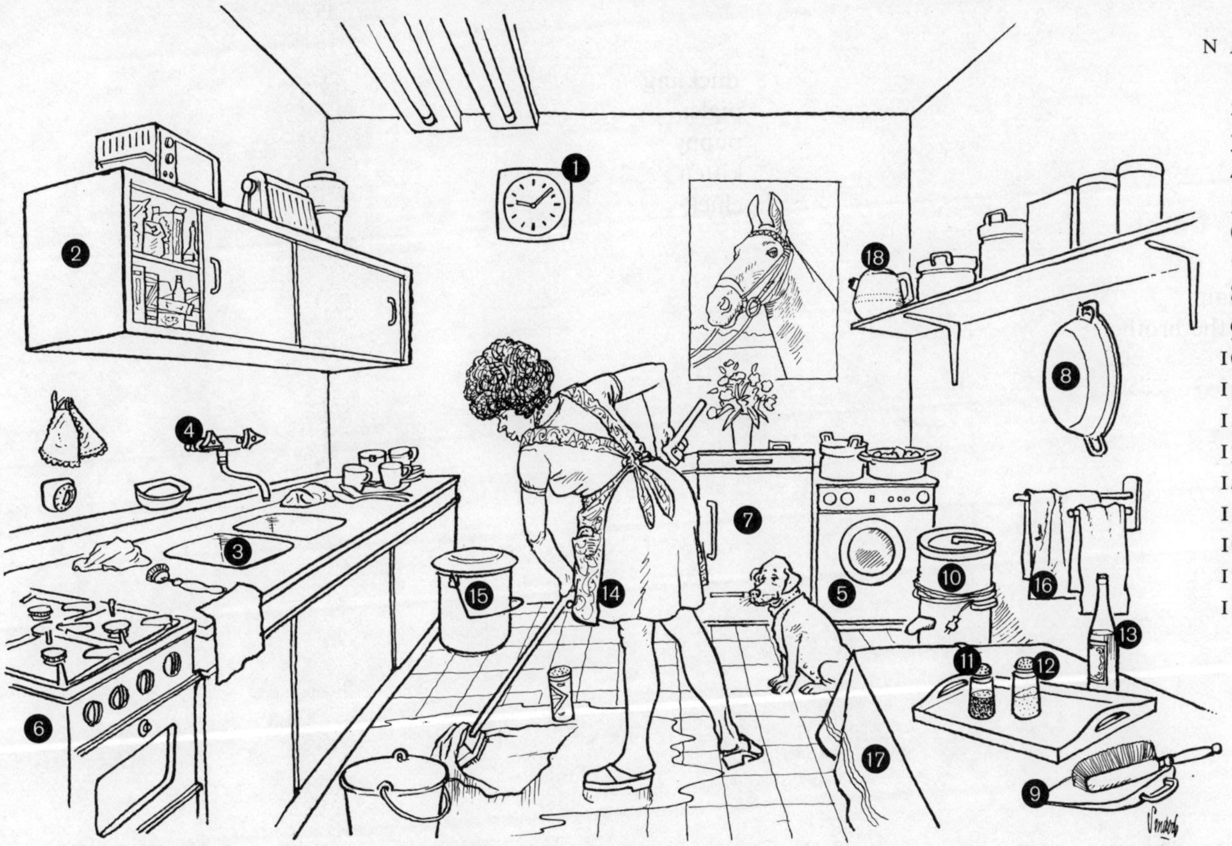

N *In the kitchen*
1 clock
2 cupboard
3 sink
4 taps
5 washing-machine
6 [gas-]cooker
7 refrigerator [fridge]
8 washing-up bowl
9 dustpan and brush
10 spin-dryer
11 pepper
12 salt
13 vinegar
14 apron
15 dustbin
16 tea-cloth/tea-towel
17 table-cloth
18 kettle

O *Animals around the house*
1 dog
2 cat
3 goose [geese]
4 duck
5 pigeon
6 cock
7 hen } chickens

P *Young animals*
duck...
pig...
dog...
cat...
hen...

P
duckling
piglet
puppy
kitten
chick

Q *Proverbs*
New brooms sweep clean.
Too many cooks spoil the broth.

31 I'm a sentence.

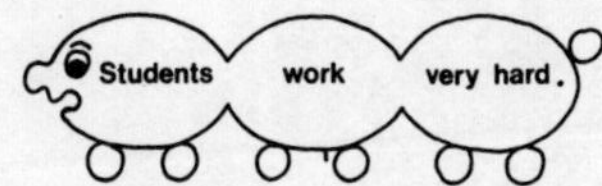

A Look at me. I'm a...
I consist of three...
My head 'students' is the...
'Work' is the...
'Very hard' is an...
The verb and adverb are the...
I have only got one predicate, therefore I'm called a...

A sentence
parts
subject
verb
adverb of manner
predicate
simple sentence

B I'm longer now and there are some more parts:
'Him' is the...
'A nice apple' is the...
'In the garden' is an...
'Yesterday' is an...
Sometimes e.g. in questions the word order is different from
the normal one. We call this...

B

indirect object
direct object
adverbial of place
adverb of time

inversion

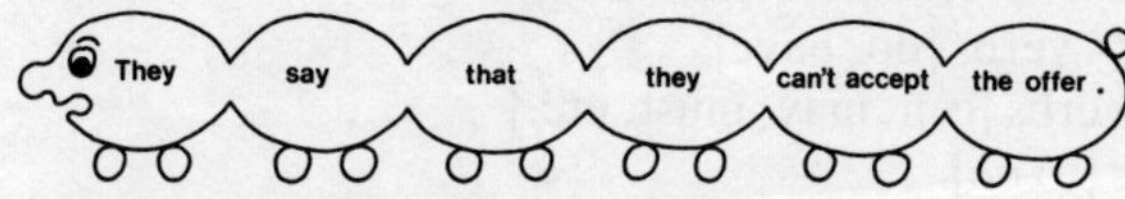

C I've got more than one predicate. I'm a:
'They say' is called the...
'They ... offer' is called the ...
The two clauses are kept together by the word 'that' which is
called a...

C compound sentence
headclause (mainclause)
subclause

conjunction

D *Parts of speech*

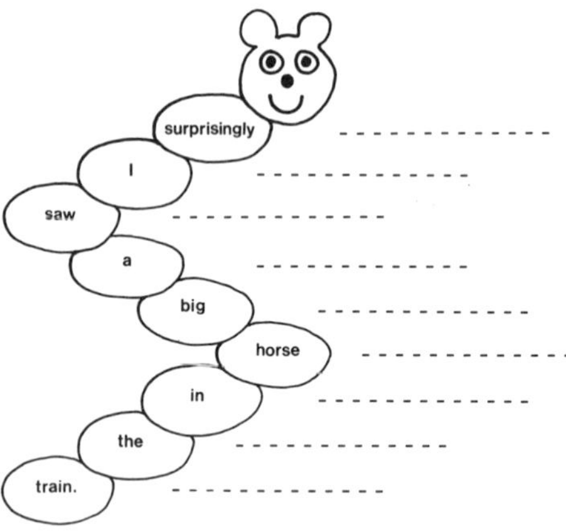

adverb
personal pronoun
verb [irregular]
article [indefinite]
adjective
noun
preposition
article [definite]
noun

E *There are several kinds of pronouns. Name the underlined*
   pronouns.
   I have never seen him.
   Who is he?
   He is my brother.
   He is the one who helped me.
   He told me this story.
   He knows everything.

E

personal pronoun
interrogative pronoun
possessive pronoun
relative pronoun
demonstrative pronoun
indefinite pronoun

F What two kinds of articles are there?

   What kinds of verbs are there?

   As to their conjugation we can divide the verbs in two
   groups viz…

   What kinds of numerals are there?

Nouns can occur either in the… or…

F definite article [the]
   indefinite article [a/an]
   main verbs [verbs of full meaning]
   auxiliary verbs [do, have]
   modal verbs [can, may, must, etc.]
   copulas [to be]
   regular verbs
   irregular verbs
   cardinal numerals [five]
   ordinal numerals [fifth]
   singular or plural or uncountable

G *Tenses*
We can distinguish two groups of tenses. Name them.

the simple tenses
the continuous tenses

Here are the most frequently used simple tenses [verb:
to help]
I help…
I helped…
I have helped…
I had helped…
I shall help…
I should help…
Here are some continuous tenses:
I am helping…
I was helping…
'He called me.' is an…
'I was called.' is a…

present tense
past tense
perfect tense
pluperfect tense
present future tense
past future tense

present continuous
past continuous
active sentence
passive sentence

H *Name the underlined verb-forms:*
I've <u>done</u> nothing.
He was <u>speaking</u> in a low voice.
<u>Smoking</u> is bad for you.

past participle
present participle
gerund [verbal noun ending in -ing]

I *Degrees of comparison*
Adjectives and adverbs can change their forms. We call
these forms the…
There are three degrees of comparison:…

degrees of comparison
the positive
the comparative
the superlative

32 The end of the journey

A John likes travelling very much. He is… of travelling   A fond

He often goes by train and then he always travels in a
first-class…   carriage/compartment

The money he has to pay for his ticket is called the…   fare

Sometimes a train reaches its destination later than expected.
Then the train has been…   delayed

This is bad when you are in a…   hurry

When John leaves the train he steps on to the…   platform

The man who carries his suitcase is the…   porter

Then he leaves the platform and walks towards the…   exit [way out]

Whenever he makes a long journey by car he has his tank
filled at a…   petrol-station/filling-station

If you want to make a journey to another country you need
a…   passport

B *Conversations on the train.*
   I took your suitcase by mistake. ... me!
   But everything is O.K. now so don't...
   I think spring is the best ... for travelling.
   Do you want a light? I think I've a box of ... in my pocket.
   I found a lot of information about this journey in a book I
   borrowed from the...
   These English measures! Could you tell me please; how long
   is an inch? A foot? And a yard? [3]

   There is a great ... between a 2nd-class and a 1st-class
   carriage.
   The first class is often preferred by businessmen and
   members of the upper...

C On his journeys John often ... at a hotel or inn.
   He rises at dawn. This means:...
   He washes, dresses and goes downstairs to have his...
   He eats two slices of ... and a ... of toast.
   Sometimes he has ... and eggs.
   Eggs can be fried or...
   After breakfast he goes to the desk to see if there is a ...
   for him.

D *Give the opposites of:*
   dawn
   sunrise
   nowadays
   to love
   top
   dead
   long ago
   noise
   often
   on purpose
   fortunately

B
excuse
worry
season
matches

library

1 inch = 2½ centimetres
1 foot = 12 inches = 30 centimetres
1 yard = 3 feet = 90 centimetres
difference

class

C stays
early in the morning
breakfast
bread and butter; round
bacon or ham
boiled
message

D
dusk
sunset
formerly
to hate
bottom
alive
lately
silence
rarely/seldom
by mistake
unfortunately

to fail
a smooth surface

to succeed
a rough surface

E After breakfast John goes to the market.
He buys a souvenir at one of the…   stalls
He takes some money from his…   purse
A lady's small bag is also called a…   purse
Banknotes are mostly kept in a…   wallet
In the background is a…   café
John is going to have a cup of … there.   coffee
You can have your coffee … or …   black or white
Suddenly one of the other hotel guests enters and they have
coffee…   together

F *Put it differently:*

He made a plan to go to the market — he intended to go to the market
s'upermarket — superstore
very glad — delighted
certificate — diploma
grown-up — adult
salary — income
profession — occupation
very tired — exhausted
What do you think of him? — What's your opinion about him?

What kind of man is he? — What sort of man is he?
It happened near my house. — It happened in the neighbourhood

G In the evening John has dinner at a restaurant.

If you want to dine at a restaurant you had better … a table. — reserve
If you can't come don't forget to … your reservation. — cancel
You ask the waiter to see the… — menu
Or you ask him what he can… — recommend
First you can have soup as a… — starter
Or a salad or anything else you… — prefer/fancy
Then follows the main course i.e…. — steak or fish
Finally, you can order a… — dessert
Normally service and V.A.T. are … in the bill. — included
If you are quite content with the service you may give the waiter some extra money This is called a… — tip
It is to be hoped that it has been a … evening. — pleasant
After dinner you can drink a nightcap or go … back to the hotel. Goodnight, sleep tight! — straight

Index

to abolish 64
above 103
abroad 4
absolutely 57
to accelerate 96
accelerator 96
acceptance 80
accident 15, 95
accommodation 20
to accompany 92
according to 68
account 114
accused 30
ace 34
ache 109
acorn 85
acquaintance 90
acquainted 91
act 43
to act 34
action 122
activity 92
actor 28, 43
actress 28, 43
to add 38
addicted 33
addition 40
address 113
to address 68
adjective 7, 132
administration 27
adolescence 59
advance 43

adverb 131, 132
advertisement 42, 115
adult 137
aerial 42
aeroplane 2
to affect 83
Africa 6
African 6
afternoon 34
after-shave 73
against 29
age 36
agreement 120
agricultural 21
agriculture 21
ahead 93
air 122
aircraft 3
airforce 120
airhostess 2
airport 2
airport buildings 2
air raid 122
to alarm 123
album 60
alcoholic 33
alderman 64
ale 35
A-level [advanced] 39
algebra 36
alive 135
alley 16
allies 122
to allow 13
almond 85
along 10
alps 10

altar 67
a.m. 35
amateur 50
ambassador 64
ambulance 94
America 6
American 6
ammunition 120
among 66
amphibian 13
amplifier 58
to amuse 41
anchor 103
ancient 76
angel 69
to angle 103
Anglican 66
Anglo-Saxon 76
angry 98
animal 11
animated film 42
ankle 109
Anno Domini 77
announcer 42
annually 85
answer 109
Antarctic 6
ante meridiem 35
antibiotic 109
antique 76
anybody 54
anyone 20
apart [from] 42
apartment 45
apartment-building 18, 45
to apologize 93
to appear 29

appetite 84
appetizing 84
to applaud 44
applicant 27
to apply for 27
to appoint 27
appointment 27
to appreciate 100
appreciation 44
April 37
apron 129
arable 22
archaeological 76
archaeology 76
archbishop 66
architect 26
Arctic 6
arena 53
arithmetic 38
arm 71
armchair 124
armistice 120
armour 75
arms 120
army 119
around 5
arrangement 92
to arrest 31
arrival 4
to arrive 4
art 28
art-critic 97
artery 110
article 100
artificial 97
artist 28
artistic 97

arts 97
as [soon as] 63
ash 85
ash-tray 94
Asia 6
Asian 6
to assist 64
assistance 117
assistant 115
astronaut 4
Athens 9
athletics 49
atmosphere 5
attack 121
to attack 121
to attend 36
attic 126
audience 41
August 37
aunt 66
Australia 6
Austria 8, 9
Austrian 8
author 28
authoress 44
authorities 46
automatic 127
autumn 37
auxiliary 76
avenue 16
aviation 4
awful 91
axe 19
bacon 135
bachelor 66
backbone 108
background 43

back-light 20
backstroke 52
backwards 96
badly 95
badminton 56
bait 103
baker 25
balance 114
balletdancer 44
balloon 4
ballot 63
ballot-box 63
ballpoint 37
ballroom 44
Baltic 7
banana 86
band 58
bank 15
Bank Holiday 87
banknote 118
banqueting-hall 78
baptism 68
baptize 68
bar 33
barber 25
bargain 28
to bark 61
barley 21
barman 32
barn 23
barometer 89
baron 79
baroness 79
baronet 79
barracks 119
barrel 35
barrister 30

basement 126
basic 63
basketball 49
bass 58
bat 51
bath 20
to bathe 87
bathing-costume 87
bathroom 73
bath-salt 73
batsman 51
battalion 121
battlefield 120
battlements 75
BBC 41
beach 70
beach-wear 70
beam 46
bean 47
bear 12
to bear 85
beard 108
beast 11
beat 61
to beat 50
beautician 73
beautiful 73
beauty-parlour 73
because 43
bedchamber 78
bedroom 125
bedspread 127
bee 61
beechnut 85
beef 22
beer 22
to beg 93

to begin 51
beginning 55
to behave 31
behind 21
Belgian 8
Belgium 8, 9
to believe 67
bell 20
belly 109
to belong 76
below 127
belt 3
berry 86
berth 103
to bet 54
to betray 122
better 28
between 7
beverage 35
beyond 127
bible 30
bicycle 16
bicycle-shed 39
bike 7
bikini 70
bill 63
biology 36
birch 85
biro 37
birthday 80
birthday cake 80
bishop 34
bit 35
bite 111
to bite 111
bitter 33
blackberry 86

blackbird 13
blackboard 36
blade 73
blanket 127
bleat 61
blessing 67
blind 107
blindman's buff 81
blinds 48
blood 110
bloom 85
blossom 85
blouse 71
to blow 73
blown up 122
blues 60
boar 23
board 32
boat 7
boatswain 103
body 2
to boil 135
bomb 122
bomber 3, 122
Bonn 9
bonnet 94
to book 7
bookcase 36
booking-office 2
book-keeper 27
bookmaker 54
bookseller 25
boot 94
booth 29
to be born 80
to borrow 46
boss 27

botany 86
both 22
bottle 84
bottle-opener 19
bottom 135
bough 85
bouquet 95
bow 101
bowl 129
bowler 52
bowtie 71
to box 53
boxing-day 87
box-number 113
B.R. [British Rail] 17
bra 74
bracelet 71
brackets 38
brain 108
brake 94
branch 27
brandy 88
brave 121
bread 22
breadth 48
to break 14
breakdown 94
breakfast 34
breast 109
breastbone 108
breaststroke 52
to breathe 5
bride 65
bridegroom 65
bridesmaid 65
bridge 15
bridle 56

briefs 74
Britain 6
British 17
Briton 76
Brittany 76
to broadcast 41
broadcast 41
broke 30
brooch 71
brook 10
broom 126
broth 130
brother 66
brown 98
brunch 35
brush 74
to brush 74
Brussels 9
brussels sprouts 47
bud 85
budget 20
to build 7
builder 47
building 2
building-company 47
building-society 46
bull 23
bullet 120
bumper 94
bunch 86
bungalow 45
bunk 103
burglar 31
burglary 31
to burn 111
to burst 81
to bury 82

bus 16
bus-driver 18
bush 11
business 27
bus-station 17
bus-stop 17
busy 95
butcher 25
butter 8
buttercup 47
butterfly stroke 52
to button down 71
to buy 2
by [heart] 40

cabaret 44
cabbage 47
cabin 103
cabinet 62
cable 102
to cackle 61
café 136
cage 12
cake 26
calendar 36
calf 23
to call up 119
calm 103
camel 12
camera 58
camera-man 98
to camp 19
campaign 77
camp-bed 19
camper 19
camping 19
camping chair 19

camping-site 20
Canada 6
canal 10
to cancel 137
candidate 39
candle 80
candlestick 125
canoe 105
cannon 120
canvas 97
cap 70
cape 71
capital 10
capsule 5
captain 2
captivity 121
to capture 121
car 7, 94
caravan 88
card 34
cardinal 132
care 3
careful 18
careless 18
cargo 101
cargo-boats 101
carnation 48
carp 104
carpenter 25
carpet 8
carriage 135
carrots 47
to carry 101
cart 21
cartoon 42
case 31
cash 114

cash-desk 116
cast 43
to cast 63
castle 16
casual 71
casualty 120
catch 52
to catch 29
cathedral 17
catholic 66
cattle 22
cattle farming 22
cauliflower 47
ceiling 26
to celebrate 80
cell 29
cellar 126
cello 59
cemetery 82
centigrade 89
central heating 128
centre 16
centre back 51
century 75
cereals 22
ceremony 65
certain 15
certificate 96
chain 20
chair 3
chairman 62
chalk 37
chalkbox 36
champion 55
chancellor 62
Chancellor of the
  Exchequer 62

to change 14
change 116
Channel 7
chapel 66
chapter 38
character 92
charcoal 97
charge 2
chart 103
to chat 33
cheap 100
to check 96
checked 72
checkmate 34
cheek 74
to cheer 50
cheerful 82
cheers 33
cheese 8
cheetah 12
chemist 25
chemistry 36
cheque 114
cheque-book 114
cherry 86
chess 34
chessboard 34
chessmen 34
chess pieces 34
chest 109
to chew 107
chicken 23
chicken-pox 110
chimney 46
chin 106
chiropody 73
chisel 26

chocolates 116
choice 28
choir 67
to choose 28
chorus 5
Christ 77
to christen 68
christian 68
Christmas 87
church 15
churchyard 65
cigar 26
cigarette 26
cigarette-machine 32
cinema 42
circle 43
circuit 55
circular 98
citizen 59
city 10
civil 120
to clap 44
class 38
classical 61
classroom 37
clean 127
to clean 48
cleaner 126
clear 91
clergyman 66
clerk 30
clever 39
client 99
cliff 87
climate 89
climbing-plant 86
cloakroom 43

clock 129
close 55
to close 35
cloth 74
clothes 28
cloudy 89
club 17
clutch 94
coach 50
coal 128
coast 87
coaster 105
coat 43
cock[erel] 23
cockle 104
cockpit 2
coconut 85
cod 104
code-number 113
coffee 84
coffin 82
cognac 88
coin 118
coke 88
colander 128
cold 91
collar 71
collar-bone 108
to collect 82
collection 113
collection-box 67
collective 85
college 37
collision 96
colonel 121
colony 64
colour 98

column 100
comb 74
to combine 22
combine harvester 22
comedy 44
comfortable 81
comic 38
comma 38
command 103
to command 121
commander 121
commander-in-chief 121
to comment 53
commentator 53
commercial 41
commercial school 37
commissioned 120
to commit 29
common 62
company 27
companion 92
comparative 133
compass 7
competitor 55
complicated 127
compound 131
comprehensive school 37
to be concerned 47
concert 41
concert hall 44
conchy 123
concrete 47
condition 16
condolences 82
conduct 31
to conduct 60
conductor 60

cone 85
to confess 30
confession 69
congratulations 81
congregation 67
conifer 85
coniferous 85
conjugation 132
conjunction 131
conker 85
to connect 44
connection 114
to conquer 77
conscientious 123
conscription 119
consequently 100
conservative 63
to consist 10
constant 109
constituency 62
constitution 63
contact 92
contact lenses 107
to contain 85
content 137
contents 48
continent 6
continually 33
continuous 43
contractor 47
contrast 42
control 83
control-tower 2
convent 68
conversation 117
conversion 133
convert 69

convey 92
convict 31
to convict 31
to coo 61
cook 103
cooker 129
cookery 36
Copenhagen 9
copse 85
copula 132
corduroy 72
cork 35
cork-screw 19
corn 8
corporal 120
correct 10
correctly 50
cosmetics 26
to cost 116
costume 87
cottage 45
cotton 27
to cough 109
counsel 30
count 79
counter 112
countess 79
country 3
country-lane 21
county 10
couple 66
courage 122
courageous 121
course 76
court 29
courtesy 93
court-martial 123

cousin 66
to cover 45
cow 23
coward 114
cowardly 121
cowboy 7
cowshed 22
crab 104
crane 101
crash 4
crawl 52
crayon 37
cream 22
creation 68
creature 104
credit 114
credit-card 114
creditor 27
creed 67
to cremate 83
crematorium 83
crew 2
cricket 49
cricket ball 51
crime 29
criminal 29
crisps 32
to croak 61
crockery 19
crocodile 11
crop 22
cross 68
to cross 15
cross-country 56
crossing 15
crow 21
to crow 61

crowd 16
crowded 17
crown 77
to crucify 68
cruel 123
cruise 102
crumpet 34
crusade 77
crusader 77
to cry 109
cubic 48
cuff 71
cultivated 48
cupboard 129
to cure 109
currency 114
curtain 48
custody 29
customer 32
customs 2
cut 111
to cut 21
cutlery 19
to cycle 20
cycle-path 20
cycle-repairer 20
cycling-track 20
cyclist 18

daffodil 48
daily 100
dairy 22
dairy farming 22
dairy products 22
daisy 47
to damage 96
damp 78

to dance 44
dance hall 44
dandelion 47
Dane 8
danger 122
dangerous 12
Danish 8
dark 78
to darn 127
darts 33
dartboard 32
dashboard 94
dating 91
dawn 135
deaf 107
to deal 34
dealer 118
dean 66
death 83
debt 114
debtor 27
decay 83
deceased 82
to deceive 60
December 37
to decide 30
deciduous 85
decimal 38
decision 121
deck 103
declaration 121
to declare 121
to decline 81
decoration 80
deed 122
deep 48
deer 14

to defeat 50
defence 121
defence system 120
to defend 119
definite 132
degree 89
delay 134
to delay 134
delicious 80
delighted 137
to deliver 113
democracy 62
demonstrative 132
denim 72
Denmark 8, 9
dentist 25
to deny 31
deodorant 73
to depart 4
department 116
department store 116
departure 4
departure lounge 2
to depend on 114
to deposit 114
to depress 109
depth 48
to derive 7
desert 12
deserter 123
design 26
to design 46
designer 72
desirable 84
desk 36
desperate 123
dessert 137

destination 17
detached 45
detail 44
determination 123
to develop 99
devil 68
diagnosis 109
diagonally 72
dial 89
to dial 113
diamond 34
dictionary 40
difference 135
different 37
differently 34
difficult 67
to dig 7
digestion 110
dinghy 105
diocese 66
diphtheria 110
diploma 137
direct 131
direction 16
directly 113
directory 113
dirty 127
disc 60
disc-jockey 60
disco[theque] 17
to discourage 122
disease 110
dishonest 31
to dislocate 110
to dismiss 27
to disperse 95
distance 17

to distinguish 99
district 62
to disturb 123
to dive 52
diver 52
to divide 16
division 40
dizzy 109
dock 30
dock area 101
dockyard 101
doctor 25
documentary 42
domestic 12
donkey 13
doorbell 116
doorhandle 127
doormat 48
doorstep 124
double-deckers 17
downstairs 116
draft 119
dragon-fly 4
draper 28
draught 35
draughts 33
draw 50
to draw 48
drawbridge 77
drawer 127
drawing 36
to dress 71
dressing-gown 74
dressing-table 74
drill 26
to drill 121
drink 33

to drink 33
to drive 16
driver 18
driving licence 96
drizzle 89
to drop 81
drug 33
drugstore 26
drum 58
drummer 59
drumstick 58
drunk 33
drunkard 33
dry 74
to dry 22
dry cleaning 74
duchess 79
duck 61
duckling 130
duke 79
dull 28
dune 10
dung 22
dungeon 78
dung-hill 22
during 3
dusk 135
dustbin 129
dustpan 129
Dutch 8
to dye 74
dynamo 20

each 7
eagle 13
ear 106
Earl 79

early 35
to earn 118
earring 71
earth 5
easel 97
easily 35
east 7
Easter 87
eastern 7
economical 118
edition 100
editor 100
education 37
eel 104
effort 80
eighteen 81
elbow 107
to elect 62
election 63
election day 63
electric 73
electrician 25
electricity 27
electronic 58
element 61
elementary school 37
elephant 11
elevator 115
Elizabethan 75
elm 85
else 55
embalming 83
to embark 102
embassy 64
to embroider 71
emerald 71
emotion 83

employee 27
employer 27
employment 27
empty 84
encourage 122
end 38
enemy 121
energy 110
to enforce 50
to engage 22
engine 2
engine-driver 18
engineer 2
England 7, 9
English 7
engraving 99
to enjoy 91
enlarge 99
enough 46
to enter 2
entertainer 41
entertainment 41
enthusiastic 50
entrance 65
envelope 113
environment 32
environmental studies 36
to equal 118
equipment 60
escalator 115
escape 123
estate-agent 45
etcetera 34
etches 99
eternal 100
Europe 6
even 55

evening 17
evening-dress 71
event 100
evergreen 85
everybody 33
everyone 33
everything 29
evidence 29
evil 68
exactly 75
to exaggerate 10
exam[ination] 40
to examine 95
examiner 40
excellent 100
exchange 114
excited 82
exclamation mark 38
to excuse 135
exhaust 94
to exhibit 99
exhibition 99
to exist 13
exit 134
to expect 89
expensive 55
expert 99
to explode 122
explorer 13
express 113
expression 10
expressionism 99
extinct 13
eye 106
eyebrow 106
eyelashes 106
eyelid 106

face 109
face-cloth 73
factory 22
to fail 39
faint 109
fair 50
to fall 89
fame 100
family 77
family name 68
famous 78
fancy 137
far 10
farmer 21
farmhand 21
farmhouse 23
farming 21
fashion 71
fashion magazine 73
fashion show 73
to fasten 3
fat 107
fate 123
fault 95
favourite 49
fearless 122
feature 42
February 37
federation 50
to feed 22
to feel 109
feeling 106
feet 48
female 44
feminine 110
fence 46
ferry 105

fertile 22
to fertilize 22
fertilizer 22
festival 60
to fetch 82
fever 107
a few 37
fiancé 65
fiancée 65
field 21
field-marshal 121
fight 120
fighter 3
fighting 120
figure 56
figure-head 101
file 26
to fill 134
film 99
to film 98
film star 28
financial 27
to find 32
fine 31
finger 107
finish 54
to finish 55
finishing line 55
Finland 8, 9
Finn 8
Finnish 8
fir 85
fire 111
to fire 27
fireplace 125
firm 27
first-aid 19

fish 13
to fish 88
fishermen 8
fishing-boat 87
fishing-gear 103
fishing-licence 103
fishing-rod 103
fit 50
to fit 16
five 38
flag 123
flagpole 123
flannel 72
flared 70
flask 84
flat 10
flight 4
float 103
floor 36
floorshow 41
flour 22
to flow 10
flower 47
flowerbed 47
flowered 70
flu 110
fluorescent 128
flute 59
fly 13
to fly 2
foal 23
fog 89
foggy 91
foliage 85
folkmusic 60
to follow 68
fond 134

font 67
food 22
fool 81
foot 7
football 49
footballer 50
football ground 50
football pitch 50
football player 50
football team 50
footpath 17
to force 27
forecast 89
forefinger 107
forehead 106
foreign 43
Foreign Office 62
Foreign Secretary 62
forest 10
fork 19
form 28
to form 38
to forget 137
to forgive 30
formal 90
formerly 135
for sale 45
fortress 77
fortunately 135
forward 52
foul play 50
foundation 46
founder 66
fountain-pen 37
fourteen 118
fox-hunting 56
fraction 38

fracture 111
to fracture 110
frame 20
France 8, 9
free 91
freedom 120
free kick 50
free style 52
to freeze 89
freighter 101
French 8
fresh 26
freshwater 103
Friday 37
fridge 129
friend 91
friendly 32
frog 12
front 37
front-door 124
frontier 7
frost 89
fruit 26
to fry 135
fuel 5
full 63
full marks 38
full stop 38
fully 32
funeral 82
funnel 101
fur 71
furniture 28
further 17
future 76
gale 89
gallery 99

gallon 33
to gallop 56
game 14
gander 23
gang-board 103
gang-way 103
garage 3
garden 47
gardener 47
garment 72
gas 128
gas-cooker 129
gas-mask 119
gate 47
to gather 92
gathering 90
gear lever 94
geese 129
general 26
generally 117
general practitioner 109
Geneva 9
gentleman 118
geography 36
geometry 36
Germany 8
Germany 8, 9
gerund 133
ghost 69
gin 88
giraffe 11
glad 92
glass 33
glasses 107
glider 3
gloomy 78
to go 6

goal 50
goal-keeper 50
God 18
gold 26
golden 65
goodbye 117
goods 28
goose 23
gooseberry 86
gospel 68
to govern 62
government 62
gown 30
gradually 107
gram 117
grammar school 37
grandfather 66
grandmother 66
grand-stand 53
grapes 86
grateful 91
grave 82
gravestone 82
graveyard 82
to graze 22
great 58
Great Britain 10
Great War 120
Greece 8, 9
Greek 8
greengrocer 25
greenhouse 47
to greet 90
greetings 92
grief 83
grocer 25
groceries 26

ground 88
ground floor 116
ground-level 126
group 5
to grow 24
to grunt 61
guard 123
guest 66
to guide 56
guilder 114
guilty 30
guitar 58
guitarist 59
gun 120
gutter 46
gymnastics 49

haddock 104
the Hague 9
hair 74
hair-brush 74
hairdresser 28
hair-piece 74
half-time 50
hall 125
ham 84
hamlet 10
hammer 26
hammock 19
handkerchief 73
handle-bars 20
to hang 126
hangar 2
hanky 73
to happen 95
happening 95

happy 65
harbour 87
hard 28
hardly 54
hare 14
harmful 22
harness 56
harp 59
to harvest 22
harvester 22
to hate 135
hawk 12
hazelnut 85
headache 109
headclause 131
headlines 100
headmaster 39
head-office 27
to heal 110
health 33
healthy 107
to hear 108
hearing 106
hearse 82
heart 34
heat 88
to heat 52
heating 128
heat-wave 102
heaven 68
heavily 89
heavy 15
hedge 21
heel 109
heir 77
helicopter 3
hell 68

hello 90
Helsinki 9
helmet 119
hen 61
herald 75
hero 123
herring 104
hi 90
high 28
high-jump 53
highly 26
high school 37
hijacker 4
hijacking 4
to hike 10
hill 10
hilly 10
hippo[potamus) 11
historian 76
historical 76
history 36
to hit 4
hitch-hiker 7
hitch-hiking 7
hobby 104
hoe 128
to hoist 121
hold 103
to hold 114
hole 127
holiday 37
holiday-maker 88
Holland 92
holy 77
Home Office 62
Home Secretary 62
honest 31

honesty 31
honey 84
hook 103
to hope 137
horizontally 72
horror 42
horse 34
horseback 7
horse-chestnut 85
hose 128
hosiery 116
hospital 95
hostel 88
hostess 82
hostile 121
hot 91
hotel 15
hour 76
household 116
hovercraft 4
to hum 61
hundred 75
hungry 12
to hunt 13
hurdling 53
hurricane 89
hurry 134
to hurt 109
husband 65
hyacinth 48
hyena 11
hygiene, hygienic 110
hymn 67
hysterical 95
ice-cream 84
ice-hockey 49
ice-rink 56

ignition-key 94
ill 107
illegal 13
illegally 31
illness 87
to imitate 97
imitation 97
immortal 100
impolite 81
important 10
impossible 10
impressed 99
impressionism 99
imprisonment 31
inch 135
to include 137
income 137
incorrect 50
incredible 67
indeed 93
indefinite 132
independent 41
index 107
Indian Ocean 7
to indicate 48
indigo 98
indirect 131
individual 49
indoor 49
industrial 27
industrious 27
industry 27
inexpensive 20
infant school 37
to infect 110
infection 109
inflammation 110

inflatable 105
to inflate 20
influenza 110
information 42
to inhale 125
injection 110
to injure 95
ink 37
inn 32
inn-keeper 32
inn sign 32
insect 86
instruction 82
instructor 50
instrument 59
instrumental 61
insurance 96
to intend 137
interest 46
interference 42
intermission 43
international 113
to interrogate 29
interrogation 29
interrogative 132
to interrupt 41
interval 43
interview 92
to interview 92
intestines 110
to introduce 63
introduction 90
Ireland 8
Irish 8
to iron 74
irregular 30
to irritate 109

isle 7
to invade 121
invasion 121
inversion 131
invitation 80
to invite 80
to involve 120
Italy 8, 9
jack 34
jacket 71
jaguar 11
jam tart 93
January 37
jar 84
javelin 53
jaw 107
jazz 60
jeans 71
jelly 80
jet 3
jeweller 26
jewellery 71
Jewish 66
job 27
jobless 27
jockey 54
joiner 28
joint 108
joke 81
journey 6
joy 82
judge 30
juice 88
juicy 86
July 37
jump 53
jumper 71

junction 15
June 37
jungle 12
junior minister 62
junior school 37
jury 30
kangaroo 12
kennel 23
kettle 129
key 127
kick-off 50
kidnapper, kidnapping 31
kidney 107
to kill 11
kilogram 117
kind 58
king 12
kiosk 88
kit 19
kitchen 125
kite 4
kitten 130
knee 70
knee-cap 108
knife 19
knight 34
to knock 15
to knock down 95
knot 102
label 117
labour 27
labourer 25
lace 72
lady 70
lager 33
lake 7
lamb 23

lamp 124
lampshade 124
lampstand 124
lance 75
land 10
to land 2
landing 3
landlord 46
landscape 99
lane 21
language 36
large 7
late 34
lately 135
latest 71
latitude 103
to laugh 33
to launch 102
lavatory 125
law 31
lawn 47
lawyer 30
to lay 54
l b w 52
to lead 60
leader 50
leaf 11
league 50
to learn 25
left back 51
leg 110
legal 31
lemon 86
lemonade 84
to lend 46
length 48
leopard 11

less 55
lesson 6
letter-box 80
lettuce 47
level 39
liberal 63
library 135
licence 96
licensed 32
lieutenant 121
life-boat 102
life-jacket 102
lift 7
to lift 33
light 16
lighter 34
lighthouse 87
lightning 89
lily 47
limb 85
lime 33
limelight 92
limited liability company 27
line 114
linen 72
liner 102
linesman 51
lion 11
lip 74
lipstick 74
liquid 128
Lisbon 9
to listen 44
litre 33
liver 107
living 26
living-room 125

load 128
to load 101
lobster 104
local 17
local call 114
loch 7
to lock 127
lodgings 32
loft 126
London 9
long-distance 17
longitude 103
long-jump 53
long player 61
long-playing record L.P. 60
long-sighted 107
lord 62
lorry 16
to lose 55
loser 50
lot 15
lotion 73
loud 61
loudspeaker 58
lounge 126
lounge bar 32
love 10
to love 135
lovely 82
low 39
to low 61
to lower 48
Ltd. 27
luggage-carrier 20
lump 55
lunch 34
lunchtime 35

lung 107
lyrics 61
mac 71
machine 60
machine-gun 120
madam 117
Madrid 9
magazine 38
magnificent 77
mail 113
main 7
mainly 17
mainsail 101
maize 21
major 121
majority 63
male 110
mammal 13
manager 27
manicure 73
mannequin 72
manner 131
manners 118
mansion 45
manual 25
manufacturer 27
manure 22
map 36
March 37
marchioness 79
margin 38
marquis 79
marriage 65
to marry 65
masculine 110
mass 67
mast 101

master 38
match 50
matches 32
matching 71
mate 103
material 47
maternity-wear 71
mathematics 36
matinée 43
matter 113
mattress 127
may 29
May 37
mayor 64
me 5
meadow 22
meal 34
to mean 4
meaning 10
means 17
measles 110
measure 135
to measure 102
meat 26
mediaeval 75
medicine 26
Mediterranean 7
to meet 32
meeting 90
melody 61
member 11
memorial 78
to mend 127
to mention 41
menu 137
merchandise 116
merchant 28

merely 44
mess 80
message 135
metal 71
metre 48
metropolis 16
mice 22
microphone 58
midday 35
middle 21
middle-aged 59
Middle-Ages 75
middle school 37
midfield men 51
midnight 35
mild 33
mile 48
military 123
milkman 25
mill 27
millinery 116
to mind 93
mine 33
minister 62
ministry 62
minus 38
minute 50
mirror 73
missile 5
mist 89
mistake 135
mixture 109
moat 77
model 72
modern 61
mole-hill 10
monarch 77

monarchy 77
monastery 68
Monday 37
money order 114
monk 68
monkey 11
month 37
monthly 100
moon 4
to moor 102
moped 16
moral 123
mortgage 46
Moscow 9
mosque 66
most 7
mostly 32
motorbike 16
motorboat 105
motorcar 82
motorcycle 16
mountain 10
mountain face 10
mountain peak 10
mountaineer 10
mourner 82
mourning 82
mouse 86
moustache 108
mouth 106
to move 20
movement 102
movie star 42
to mow 47
mudguard 94
multiplication 40
to multiply 38

mumps 110
municipal council 64
municipality 64
murder 31
murderer 31
muscle 107
museum 15
music 36
musical 44
music-hall 17
musician 28
mussel 104
mutton 22

nail 74
nail-brush 74
nail-file 74
nail-scissors 74
nail-varnish 74
namely 34
narrow 16
nation 120
native 6
nave 67
to navigate 103
navigation 103
navy 120
near 12
neat 127
necessary 118
necessity 31
neck 71
necklace 71
to need 19
needle 109
needlework 36
to neigh 61

neighbourhood 137
nephew 66
nerve 107
nervous 110
Netherlands 8, 9
newsflash 41
newspaper 38
newsreel 42
nice 74
nicely 33
niece 66
night-club 44
nightdress 71
night-wear 70
nil 50
nobility 79
noblemen 79
nobody 63
noise 135
noisy 61
non-commissioned 120
non-iron 74
noon 35
normally 137
Normandy 76
Normans 76
north 7
North Sea 7
Norway 8, 9
Norwegian 8
nose 73
nostrils 106
notice 32
notional 132
noun 132
novel 100
novelist 100

November 37
nowadays 64
number 34
to number 38
nun 68
nunnery 68
nurse 25
nursery 126
nursery school 36
nut 32
nylon 72

oak 85
oar 104
oath 30
oats 21
object 76
objection 63
objector 123
to observe 52
occasion 80
occupation 137
occur 132
ocean 7
o'clock 17
October 37
octopus 104
of course 46
offence 29
offender 50
offer 80
office 18
officer 15
official 50
off switch 42
often 5
oil 83

oil-painting 99
ointment 109
old-age pensioner 59
old-fashioned 73
Olympic Games 53
oncoming 96
one 6
onion 47
onlooker 94
opener 19
opera 44
operahouse 44
operate 95
operation 95
operator 114
opinion 137
opponent 50
opposite 18
optician 25
oral 39
orange 86
orange juice 88
orchard 86
orchestra 60
order 13
to order 33
ordinal 132
ordinary 113
Ordinary level [O-level] 39
organ 59
organisation 13
organist 59
orphan 83
Oslo 9
ostrich 12
outdoor 49
outline 88

outsider 54
outsize 71
oval 98
overcast 89
overdraft 114
overtake 96
overthrow 120
overwhelmed 82
to owe 27
owner 32
oxygen 5
oyster 104
pack 34
pack of hounds 56
packet 125
page 38
pain 109
painful 110
painless 110
paint 97
painter 25
painting 26
pair 26
palace 18
palette 98
palm 107
pan 19
panties 74
pants 74
paper 100
parachute 4
parade 70
parade-ground 119
paradise 68
paragraph 38
paratroopers 122
parcel 81

pardon 93
parents 95
Paris 9
parish 66
to park 96
Parliament 62
parrot 125
parson 68
parsonage 68
part 5
partially 107
participle 133
partner 92
party 63
to pass 3
passage 125
passenger 2
passenger-ship 101
passport 134
patient 109
pattern 72
pavement 15
pawn 34
pay 26
to pay 117
pea 47
peace 120
peach 86
peanut 85
pear 86
pedal 20
to pedal 20
pedestrian 15
peer 79
peerage 79
peg 126
pelvis 108

pen 26
penalty kick 50
pence 118
pencil 37
penny 118
people 2
pepper 129
per 20
percent 10
perch 104
perfect 133
to perform 43
performance 43
perfume 74
perhaps 55
period 59
permission 20
permit 103
person 29
personal 132
to perspire 107
pest 22
pet 12
petrol-station 134
pew 67
phone 114
photo 98
photo-finish 55
to photograph 13
photographer 98
photography 98
physics 36
pianist 59
piano 59
to pick up 91
picnic 84
picnic-basket 84

picture 98
picture postcard 114
picturesque 98
pie 32
piece 71
pier 87
pig 23
pigeon 61
piglet 23
pike 104
pill 109
pillar-box 113
pillow 127
pillow-case 127
pillow-slip 127
pilot 2
pin 109
pincers 26
to pinch 117
pine 85
pineapple 86
pink 98
pint 33
pipe 125
pistol 120
pitch 51
pitched 46
pity 83
to pity 83
plaice 104
plain 72
plane [schaaf] 26
plane 3
planet 5
plant 86
to plant 47
plantation 86

to plaster 26
plasterer 26
plate 19
platform 134
platinum 71
platoon 121
player 32
playground 17
play school 37
playwright 44
to plead 30
pleasant 137
pleasure 80
plough 22
to plough 22
plug 48
plum 86
plumber 26
plump 107
to plunge 52
pluperfect 133
plural 132
plus 33
p.m. 35
pneumonia 110
to poach 13
poacher 13
P.O.B. 113
pocket 71
poem 5
poet 100
poetry 100
poison 31
poisonous 12
Poland 8, 9
Pole 8
pole-vault 53

police 29
policeman 15
police-station 29
Polish 8
polite 90
political 63
politician 64
politics 64
polling-station 63
pool 10
poor 39
pop 58
pop concert 58
Pope 66
pop group 5
poplar 85
poppy 47
popular 58
pork 22
porridge 22
port 102
porter 134
portholes 101
portrait 99
Portugal 8, 9
Portuguese 8
positive 133
to possess 118
possessive 132
possible 10
to post 112
postage 113
postal order 114
postcard 88
poster 63
postman 25
postmaster 113

post meridiem 35
post office 112
post [office] box 113
potatoes 21
potion 109
potter 28
pottery 76
poulterer 26
pound 114
to pour 89
poverty 31
P.O.W. 123
powder 109
powder-puff 74
power station 27
practical 37
practice 21
to practise 22
prawn 104
to pray 67
prayer 67
precious 71
predatory 11
predicate 131
to prefer 135
preference 117
prehistory 76
première 43
to prepare 80
preposition 132
to prescribe 109
present 33
to present 90
to preserve 13
president 77
to pretend 34
previously 90

prey 11
price 117
to price 20
primary school 36
Prime Minister 62
prince 77
princess 77
principal 24
to print 99
printed matter 113
prison 31
prisoner 78
private 113
prize 55
probably 90
probation 31
problem 35
process 83
procession 82
to produce 27
producer 42
product 21
profession 25
professional 50
professor 28
profit 118
programme 41
to prohibit 20
promenade 88
pronoun 132
property 46
prophet 66
to propose 81
prose 100
prosecution 30
protection 122
proverb 14

province 64
psalm 67
pub 17
pub clock 32
public 46
publican 32
public bar 32
public house 32
to publish 100
publisher 100
to pull 48
pulpit 67
pulse 109
pump 20
puncture 20
to punish 31
punishment 31
pupil 36
puppy 130
purple 98
purpose 135
purse 136
to push 117
to put [off] 40
to put up 20
pyjamas 70

to quack 61
quality 117
quart 33
quarter 16
queen 34
question 20
question mark 38
to queue up 116
quickly 81
quiet 61

quite 137

race 54
race-horse 54
race-track 54
racing 53
radar 4
radio 4
rafter 46
rail 17
railing 101
railway 17
to rain 89
rainbow 98
raincoat 71
to raise 22
rake 128
ram 23
rank 62
rarely 135
rat 22
rate 46
rate of exchange 114
rather 33
razor 73
to reach 63
reaction 50
ready-made 74
rear 20
rear-view 94
reason 10
reasonably 70
rebound 58
to recapture 123
to receive 42
receiver 42
reception 42

to recognize 29
to recommend 137
record 31
to record 60
recorder 59
record-player 60
to recover 95
recreation 17
rectangular 98
rector 66
rectory 68
red 98
reed 45
reel 127
referee 50
refreshing 35
refreshment 88
refrigerator 129
refusal 81
to refuse 28
regards 81
regiment 121
to register 113
registration 96
regular 102
to regulate 16
rehearsal 43
to reign 64
rein 56
to reject 63
relative 66
relatively 57
to release 31
relief 123
religion 66
religious 123
religious studies 36

to remain 3
to remember 92
to remove 128
rent 46
to repair 3
to repay 46
to repeat 93
replete 14
to reply 80
reporter 53
to represent 62
representative 63
reptile 13
republic 77
to request 80
to resemble 92
reservation 137
to reserve 7
resort 87
responsible 100
rest 123
restaurant 15
restless 12
result 50
retailer 118
return 81
to reverse 96
reversed 114
revolution 61
revolver 120
revolving door 115
reward 55
Rhine 7
rhino[ceros] 11
rhyme 89
rhythm 60
rib 108

ride 5
to ride 24
rider 56
riding 53
riding-boots 56
riding-crop 56
rifle 119
right back 51
right of way 16
ring 26
to ring 116
rise 26
to rise 135
river 8
road-manager 60
roadside 7
road-sign 16
robber 31
robbery 31
robin 13
rock 102
rock 'n roll 58
roll 80
roller 74
Roman 66
Rome 9
roof 45
rook 34
root 85
rope 102
rose 48
rough 136
roundabout 16
rover 10
to row 104
rowing 49
rowing-boat 104

royal 77
rubbish 128
ruby 71
rucksack 19
rudder 101
rude 80
rugby 50
rugger 50
ruins 77
rule 50
to rule 62
rummy 34
runway 2
rush 17
Russia 8, 9
Russian 8

to sack 27
sad 114
saddle 20
safari 13
safari-suit 71
safe 5
to sail 49
sailing-ship 101
sailor 103
saint 69
salad 137
salary 26
sale 116
salesman 25
salmon 104
salt 129
saltwater-fish 104
to salute 121
same 50
sandwich 32

satchel 36
satin 71
saucepan 19
saucer 19
sausage 26
savannah 13
to save 102
savings bank 114
saxophone 59
saying 44
scales 117
scarecrow 21
scarf 74
scarlet fever 110
scene 43
scenery 43
school 36
school-bag 36
school building 15
science 37
scissors 19
to score 50
Scotland 7
scratch 111
screen 42
screwdriver 19
sculpting 98
sculptor 28
sculpture 97
sea-fish 103
sea-level 103
sea-map 103
seamen 103
seashore 87
seasick 102
seasickness 102
seaside 87

season 135
seat 3
seat-belt 3
second 54
secondary modern school 37
secondary school 36
secret 63
secretary 27
section 121
sedative 110
seed 21
to seem 34
selection 71
self-service 117
to sell 26
to send 42
sender 113
senior 59
senior high school 37
sentence 31
to sentence 31
sentry 119
to separate 7
sergeant 120
sergeant-major 120
serious 29
sermon 67
serve 53
service 46
[T.V.] set 42
to set [up] 55
settee 124
several 37
to sew 127
sewing-machine 127
sex 135
sexton 66

shade 88
shadow 88
to shake 90
shaking 81
shape 98
shark 13
sharp 111
to shave 73
shaving-brush 73
shaving-cream 73
shaving-soap 73
shed 125
sheep 23
sheet 126
shell 119
shelter 122
sherry 8
shield 75
shilling 118
shin 108
to shine 88
ship 101
shipwrecked 102
shire 64
shirt 74
shivery 109
shock 95
to shock 95
shop-assistant 25
shopkeeper 25
shopping-area 16
shopping-bag 115
shopping-centre 16, 18
shop window 29
short 27
short-sighted 107
short-sleeved 74

shoulder 21
to shout 50
show 41
to show 44
shower 20
shrimp 104
shrub 85
to shuffle 34
to shut 48
sick 102
side 38
side-street 17
siege 122
sieve 128
to sift 128
sight 18
sign 32
to sign 63
signature 113
silence 135
silk 71
silly 81
silver 65
simple 127
singer 28
single 61
singular 132
sink 129
Sir 79
sitting-room 126
six 17
size 48
to skate 53
sketch 99
skill 73
skilled 27
skin 107

skin-diving 49
skirt 71
skull 108
skyscraper 16
slapstick 42
slave 64
slavery 64
to sleep 22
sleeping-bag 19
sleeve 60
slice 135
slim 72
slim-fitting 70
slope 10
to slow down 57
slowly 12
slum 16
small 10
small-pox 110
smart 71
to smell 74
smoke 125
to smoke 33
smooth 136
snake 13
to sneeze 109
snow 89
soap 26
soccer 49
sociable 32
social 90
sock 74
socket 48
soft 88
soil 22
sold 28
soldier 119

solemn 83
solicitor 46
somebody 25
someone 20
something 31
sometimes 7
song 5
sorrow 83
sorry 81
sort 13
S.O.S. 102
so that 55
soul 60
soup 137
sour 86
south 7
South America 6
Southpole 6
to sow 22
space 5
spacecraft 4
space-helmet 5
spaceman 5
space rocket 4
space-station 5
space-suit 5
spade 128
spades 34
Spain 8, 9
Spaniard 8
Spanish 8
spasmodic 109
to speak 27
special 79
special delivery 113
specially 20
spectator 53

speech 132
speed 55
speedometer 94
to speed up 57
to spend 73
spice 83
spin-dryer 129
spine 108
spinster 66
spirit 69
spirits 33
to spoil 130
spoke 35
sponge 73
to sponsor 55
spoon 19
sport 49
sportscar 96
spot 14
spotlight 58
spotted 70
to sprain 110
to spread 84
spring 37
springtime 85
to sprinkle 68
spy 123
squadron 121
square 78
squash 56
squeamish 109
squire 79
squirrel 86
stable 23
stadium 53
staff 121
stag 23

stage 43
stage-manager 43
stained glass 65
staircase 124
stairs 124
stall 88
stalls 43
stamp 112
to stamp 117
stamp-machine 112
stand 53
to stand 7
star 42
starboard 103
start 3
to start 4
state 83
statement 29
station 15
stationer 26
statue 78
stay 92
to stay 135
steak 137
to steal 31
steamer 101
steel 27
steep 102
steeple 65
to steer 103
steering-wheel 94
stern 101
steward 103
still life 99
sting 111
stirrup 56
stock 117

Stockholm 9
stocking 74
stomach 84
stone 47
stool 32
to store 103
storey 17
storm 89
stormy 102
story 132
stout 107
straight 137
to strain 128
straw 14
strawberry 86
streamer 80
streetcar [Am] 16
to stretch 52
strike 28
to strike 28
striker 51
strip 46
striped 70
stroke 52
student 20
studio 28
study 76
to study 36
stupid 39
style 99
subclause 131
sub-divided 121
subject 37
submarine 105
subtitle 43
to subtract 38
subtraction 40

suburb 16
to succeed 136
success 58
such 33
suddenly 136
suede 72
to suffer 95
suffrage 63
sugar 22
sugar-beet 21
suit 71
suitable 71
suitcase 134
sum 38
summer 87
sunburnt 87
Sunday 37
sunny 89
sunshade 87
sunstroke 87
suntan 87
superior 121
superlative 133
supermarket 137
supper 34
to support 50
supporter 50
sure 43
surface 10
surf-board 87
surfer 87
surfing 88
surgeon 95
surname 68
surprise 82
surrender 121
to surrender 121

surroundings 16
to swallow 109
to swear 30
to sweat 107
Swede 8
Sweden 8, 9
Swedish 8
to sweep 130
sweet 80
to swerve 96
to swim 7
swimming-cap 70
swimming-pool 17
swimming-trunks 87
Swiss 8
to switch on 128
to switch off 48
Switzerland 8, 9
sword 75
synagogue 66
system 37

table-cloth 129
table-lamp 128
table-tennis 49
tail 2
tailor 28
tailor-made 74
to take after 92
to take care of 3
to take off 3
take off 3
talcum-powder 73
to talk 64
talkative 32
tambourine 59
tame 14

tank 119
tanker 105
tap 129
tart 84
task 3
to taste 35
tax 46
taxi 16
taxi-driver 25
tea-cloth (-towel) 129
teacher 25
team 50
team sport 49
technical school 37
technique 99
teenager 59
teeth 73
teetotaller 33
telegram 112
telephone 112
telephone box [booth] 29
telephone call 112
telephone directory 112
telephone kiosk 112
television 41
to tell 54
temperature 89
temple 8
tempo 61
ten 118
tenant 46
tennis 56
tense 76
tent 19
tent-peg 19
tent-pole 19
terraced 45

territory 77
testament 67
to testify 30
tetanus 110
text 38
Thames 7
thankful 91
thatch 45
thatched 45
theatre 43
theft 31
themselves 118
theoretical 37
therefore 15
thermometer 89
thick 89
thief 29
thigh 109
thigh-bone 108
thimble 127
thin 107
to think 35
third 54
thirsty 12
thirty 89
thousand 117
thread 127
thrifty 118
thriller 42
throat 109
throne 77
through 13
to throw 22
thumb 107
thunder 89
thunderstorm 89
ticket 2

to tickle 109
tide 103
tie 71
tiger 12
tight 70
tights 74
tile 26
tiler 26
till 40
tiller 101
timber 46
time 35
time chart 76
time-table 17
tin-opener 19
tip 137
tipsy 34
tire 20
tired 137
tissue 73
title 79
toast 81
tobacconist 26
today 40
toe 117
together 18
toilet 20
toilet bag 74
tomb, tombstone 82
tomorrow 40
tongue 107
tonight 41
tooth 73
tooth-brush 73
tooth-paste 73
torch 19
torn 127

tote 54
touch 92
to touch 3
tourist 88
tournament 75
towards 134
towel 73
tower 18
town 15
town-council 64
town-hall 15
tractor 21
trade 25
tradesman 25
traffic 15
traffic-jam 95
traffic-light 15
traffic-warden 94
tragedy 44
trainer 50
training 50
traitor 123
tram 16
tranquillizer 110
transept 67
to translate 40
to transmit 42
transmitter 42
to transpire 107
transport 17
to travel 7
travellers' cheques 114
trawler 104
tray 128
treacherous 122
treason 123
treasury 62

treatment 73
treaty 120
tree-trunk 85
tremendously 91
trial 30
triangular 98
trifle 84
trip 6
trombone 59
tropics 14
to trot 56
troubles 10
trousers 71
trouser-legs 70
trout 104
trumpet 59
trunk 85
trunk call 113
truth 30
to try 7
T-shirt 71
tuba 59
tug 105
tulip 48
tune 61
to turn 80
to turn off 48
Turk 8
Turkey 8, 9
Turkish 8
turnip 47
turret 77
tweed 71
twice 81
twig 85
to twitter 61
type 37

typewriter 127
typist 25
tyre 20
umpire 52
uncle 66
unconscious 95
underground 17
underground-station 16
underlined 35
to understand 43
understood 43
underwear 116
unexpected 82
unexpectedly 81
unfortunately 135
ungrateful 91
unhappy 68
unhealthy 78
uniform 121
unit 121
to unite 64
united 6
universe 5
university 37
unjust 31
unkind 91
unless 31
unload 101
unnecessary 118
unopened 85
unsportsmanlike 13
up-hill 10
upholsterer 28
upside-down 80
upstairs 116
to use 60
useful 22

usual[ly] 33
vacancy 27
vaccinated 110
vacuum 126
valley 10
value 97
van 16
vase 125
Vatican 66
vegetables 47
vein 107
velvet 72
verb 3
verger 66
vertically 72
vessel 102
vicar 66
vicarage 68
victory 121
Vienna 9
view 48
Vikings 76
village 10
vine 86
vinegar 129
vineyard 86
violent 89
violet 98
violin 59
viscount 79
viscountess 79
visiting hour 95
visitor 99
viz. 34
vocal 61
volleyball 53
volume 42

volunteer 119
vomit 102
vote 63
voter 63
voyage 6
wages 26
waist 71
waiter 44
waitress 44
to wake [up] 126
wall 26
wallet 136
war 120
wardrobe 127
warehouse 101
warm 35
warning 50
Warsaw 9
wartime 5
to wash 74
wash-basin 128
washing 127
washing-line 126
washing-machine 127
washing-up bowl 129
wasp 13
to waste 118
wastepaper basket 36
to watch 13
to water 128
water-bus 105
water-polo 49
waterproof 71
waterskiing 88
wave 74
way 7
weapon 120

to wear 70
wearing 70
weary 10
weather 4
weather-cock 65
wedding 65
wedding-cake 65
wedding-ring 65
to weed 47
week 29
weekly 100
to weep 109
weeping willow 85
to weigh 117
weight 117
welcome 102
well-known 7
west 7
western 7
wet 78
whale 13
what 2
wheat 21
wheel 20
to wheel 128
wheelbarrow 128
whether 30
which 6
while 10
whiskey 8
whist 34
to whistle 50
Whit Monday 87
who 2
wholesale 118
whooping-cough 110
whose 41

wicket 52
wide 48
wide-brimmed 71
widow 83
widower 83
width 48
wife 65
wig 30
Wight 7
wild 14
wildlife 13
willow 85
to win 50
wind 89
wind-breaker 87
window 29
window-cleaner 48
windscreen 94
windscreen-wiper 94
Windsor 77
wine 8
wine-cellar 126
winner 50
to wipe 48
wire 112
wireless 42
wiring 26
to withdraw 114
witness 29
witness-box 30
wolf 12
wonderful 91
wood 8
woodland 85
woodwork 36
woody 85
wool 8

word order 131
to work 26
worker 25
working-day 88
workman 26
works 27
world 6
world record 55
World War I 120
worn 70
to worry 135
worse 39
worship 67
worth 114
wound 110
wounded 120
to wrap [up] 117
wreath 82
wreck 102
wrestling 49
wrist 71
to write 38
writer 100
writing-paper 113
xylophone 59
yard 135
yard-stick 26
yellow 114
yesterday 131
yet 10
young 20
youngster 71
youth-hostel 20
zebra 11
zebra-crossing 15
zero 89
zoo 12